'A truly fascinating study. It shows why and how i
difference, and why background is not everything.
universities pause, because how they treat student
not always in the ways that they assume.

**Baroness Alison Wolf, Sir Roy Griffiths Professor of Public Sector
Management, King's College London**

'These fascinating interviews with 15 young men as they progress through
their university experience suggest ways of resolving the age-old problem
of under-achievement by white working-class boys. A must-read study.'

**Carol V. Robinson, Dr Lee's Professor of Physical Chemistry,
University of Oxford**

White Working-Class Boys

For the 15 young men whose life stories stimulated the writing of this book.

White Working-Class Boys
Teachers matter

Mary-Claire Travers

is an imprint of

First published in 2017 by the UCL Institute of Education Press, 20 Bedford Way, London WC1H 0AL

www.ucl-ioe-press.com

British Library Cataloguing in Publication Data:
A catalogue record for this publication is available from the British Library

ISBNs
978-1-85856-840-9 (paperback)
978-1-85856-841-6 (PDF eBook)
978-1-85856-842-3 (ePub eBook)
978-1-85856-843-0 (Kindle eBook)

Every effort has been made to trace copyright holders and to obtain their permission for the use of copyright material. The publisher apologizes for any errors or omissions and would be grateful if notified of any corrections that should be incorporated in future reprints or editions of this book.

The opinions expressed in this publication are those of the author and do not necessarily reflect the views of the UCL Institute of Education.

Typeset by Quadrant Infotech (India) Pvt Ltd
Printed by CPI Group (UK) Ltd, Croydon, CR0 4YY

Cover image © ARENA Creative/Shutterstock.

Contents

List of tables and figures

About the author

Dr Mary-Claire Travers developed an interest in the educational achievement of white working-class boys during the late 1970s, when teaching white working-class children in very deprived parts of south London. It left her with a strong sense that a different approach was required to lift the academic achievements of these students.

Mary-Claire undertook a PhD at King's College, London, and worked in the Department of Education and Professional Studies there. Currently, she is involved, on a part-time basis, in a project on Best Practice in Setting, headed by Professor Becky Francis at UCL Institute of Education and funded by the Education Endowment Foundation.

Mary-Claire's research on white working-class boys' academic achievement has aimed to establish the multifaceted variables that enable white working-class males to achieve academic success. It has also provided unique perspectives on the issues faced by white working-class boys in their education, and has explored insightful potential solutions to the problems they experience. Her research is ongoing.

Acknowledgements

Firstly, I must acknowledge the young men who took part in this study; they gave so generously of their time over almost five years. Their life stories form the basis for this book and I am indebted to them.

I also wish to acknowledge Professor Meg Maguire, my PhD supervisor. It was her suggestion that I write this book and it was her unwavering belief in me, as well as her continuous encouragement, advice, and guidance, that ensured that it was completed. I cannot thank her enough.

My husband, Glen, who has consistently shown great support, encouragement, and tolerance, and generously shared his IT skills, must be acknowledged and thanked. My children, Natalie, Jessica, and Nicholas, have offered constant encouragement. Natalie and Jessica have also given generously of their time proofreading several chapters and Natalie formatted the bibliography. Thank you.

To my extended family and friends who have offered encouragement and support, and shown endless patience – thank you.

I cannot forget to acknowledge all those at Trentham Books who willingly worked to see the draft through to publication, especially Gillian Klein, who believed in the project from the beginning and constantly offered valuable advice and encouragement.

Foreword

Professor Meg Maguire

Some time ago, Mary-Claire Travers gave me a copy of *Strangers in Paradise*. It is an account of 24 predominantly male academics who had come from working-class families (Ryan and Sackrey, 1984). In the introduction to their book, Ryan and Sackrey wrote that life was 'shaped in society by things and ideas, among the most important of the latter, the myth that there is an escape from the influence of social class on a person's life experience' (p. 13). Their argument was that the myth of upward mobility was largely 'a grand lie' (p. 317). Their data was collected from individuals in the USA who had moved from a working-class background to become college professors and who all generally testified to the power of this lie.

In some ways, this book contains a story that mirrors the one being told in *Strangers in Paradise*. At the start of *White Working-Class Boys: Teachers matter*, the statistics that are reviewed still speak powerfully to the way in which working-class people are expected and predicted to do badly, to 'under-achieve', and to take up subordinate positions in the social world that match their 'attainment' – their just desserts. The problem is, if they did not do this, what would happen to all those more privileged people who expect and demand their place at the top table? So, if social mobility is a chimera, what can be done to shift persistent and pernicious class inequality? Perhaps one thing that complex biographical narratives can do is tell another story and ask a different set of questions.

In this book, Mary-Claire Travers looks at a small number – and the numbers are still extremely small – of those working-class men who have been 'successful' at school and have attended various universities. She explores some of the factors that have contributed towards these achievements and she describes the ways in which family background and early school experiences, as well as encounters with significant teachers, have contributed to the young men's accounts of how they have bucked the trend of white, male, working-class under-achievement. However, this book is not an account of what can be done to ensure that more white working-class males are supported in attending university; challenging power, status, and privilege that is so well entrenched is a massive question for those concerned with matters of social justice. However, books can highlight unfairness and injustice.

Many commentators have pointed out that education cannot 'compensate' for the structural and material injustices that characterize our social world. Without a real and concerted effort to provide decent housing, quality health provision, good employment prospects, and a fair wage (and most families trapped in poverty are working households), education on its own is not going to be able to do more than dent the old, old problem of social class injustice. One of the more disheartening aspects of the stories recounted in this book is that the young men all remember practices in their schools that marginalized, rejected, or did violence to other young working-class males – either through their structures and internal organization or through the disparagement of working-class children more generally. This book continues the work that concentrates on the ways in which working-class young people are often subordinated and sidelined in their encounters with the school system. While the men in Travers's work do not seem to have experienced a great degree of estrangement and disillusionment with their higher education experiences, their stories are not yet done.

White Working-Class Boys: Teachers matter is a reminder then of what educational provision is still failing to do. Education is important and it can be a site for contesting the status quo and for questioning the rules by which we live and work – although not on its own. This book helps to keep some of the age-old questions on the agenda – who gets what and why – and it does so in an engaging yet critical way.

Meg Maguire
King's College London

Preface

The worst thing ... we as a culture do about our teenagers is that we only seem to discuss them in negative terms. What they can't do, what they aren't achieving. Why have we allowed this to happen?

(Patrick Ness cited in Flood, 2012)

I have been interested in the educational achievement of white working-class boys since the late 1970s. My time teaching white working-class children in very deprived parts of south London, compared with other experiences in England and Australia teaching more privileged students, left me feeling that something different had to be tried to lift the academic achievements of these students. There was then, and there continues to be, a rump of some 20–25 per cent of young people in England who leave school with limited qualifications (Maguire, 2009). White working-class boys have always been disproportionately represented in this cohort (Strand, 2014).

The under-achievement of white working-class boys in England is well documented and they remain the lowest academic achievers at the age of 16 for any socio-economic class grouping (Strand, 2014). To date, most research that has focused on white working-class boys has dealt with their failure to engage with education and the reasons for this (Hills *et al.*, 2010; Willis, 1977).

In contrast, this book has taken a different approach to a topic that is often reviewed from a problem-based stance. There is little research that explores academically successful white boys from a working-class background and the multifaceted variables that contribute to their success. The intention in this book is to provide detailed, critical, and socially contextualized accounts of the life experiences of 15 academically successful white working-class young men. The research data that forms the basis of this study was gathered from three in-depth semi-structured interviews conducted with the young men over the period of their university undergraduate studies. Eight of the men attended post-1992 or modern universities (originally polytechnics or colleges of further education) and seven attended elite universities (the oldest universities in the country).

The young men were not immune to the adverse situations that many working-class students face educationally, but they had also had compensatory factors in their lives that enabled them to experience academic success. They all came from families who valued education, although most of their siblings did not go on to higher education, and this speaks of the young men's agency. They all experienced academic success early and this seems to have stood them in good stead when, later in their school careers, many of them found themselves in challenging secondary schools and situations. Mentor teachers played an important if not fundamental role in the academic lives of the participants; progression to university would in many cases not have happened without these mentors, who played an instrumental role in the academic trajectories of the young men.

The young men's stories tell of achievement *against the odds*: all needed persistence, resilience, and sheer determination at various stages in their school and university careers. It is little wonder then that so few young white working-class men manage to get through the net each year. Despite the rhetoric about improving opportunities for those who are less well off, society by and large continues to reproduce itself.

An introduction

Education is a social achievement for which some of us are more prepared than others.

(Evans, 2006: 13)

Chapter 1 provides a contextual frame for my book that is concerned with white working-class boys' under-achievement in schools in England and the long-standing correlation between class and under-achievement. However, unlike most previous research, I adopt a novel approach to this situation by focusing on a more positive account – by exploring the multifaceted variables that contributed to the academic *success* of 15 white working-class young men who were, with one exception, the first in their families to go to university. While there have been some researchers who have explored working-class educational success (Ingram, 2009; Ingram, 2011; Reay *et al.*, 2009; Rollock, 2006), the area of white working-class boys' educational success remains largely under-researched.

For some time, the main focus has been on white working-class boys' lack of educational success. This has been and is a matter of concern not just for educators and academics (Reay *et al.*, 2009; Strand, 2014; Willis, 1977) but also for politicians (House of Commons Education Committee, 2014), and rightly so, because white working-class boys are the lowest academic performers of any ethnic group at age 16 (Centre for Social Justice, 2013; Strand, 2014; Sutton Trust, 2016). Figure 1.1 provides an overview of the attainment of all free school meal (FSM) students at Key Stage 4 (aged 16) in the academic year 2013/14. A standard indicator of socio-economic disadvantage is eligibility for free school meals, so I use FSM as a shorthand for the students in my cohort. What the figure reveals is that white British FSM boys are the lowest performers of any group in both General Certificate of Secondary Education (GCSE) and the English Baccalaureate (EBacc). This is a serious issue because academic achievement at GCSE level is critical: if young people fail to achieve well at this stage of their educational trajectory, their subsequent life chances are often limited (Dilnot, 2016; Wolf, 2011).

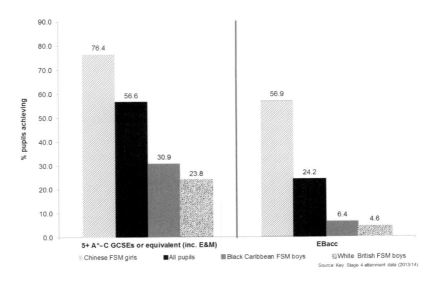

Figure 1.1: Attainment at Key Stage 4 by key groups
Source: DfE, *GCSE and Equivalent Attainment by Pupil Characteristics, 2013–14*

My study

My approach focuses on the factors that contributed to the academic success of the young men who participated in my study. In my research design, I take 'academic success' to mean successfully negotiating the school system and gaining entrance to university. Academic success means different things to different people and it can mean different things to one individual at different times in his or her life. Nevertheless, someone who has successfully negotiated the school system and gained entrance to university is generally considered to be academically successful (Brown *et al.*, 2011).

My research uncovered a multitude of factors that led to the academic success of the young men, such as the institutional habitus of the schools attended, the positive influence of a teacher or teachers, and personal attributes shown by the young men, which included qualities of perseverance, motivation, and good study skills. The young men were agentic in their educational progression and they worked hard at achieving their aims, although their educational journeys were littered with obstacles as the extended extract below elucidates:

> I was in the bottom set for everything, I didn't really do anything,
> I just messed about ... when it got closer to the exams [GCSE]
> because I was the best in the bottom sets I wanted to go up so

that I could do the higher ones [subjects] so that I could actually get at least a try, but they wouldn't have any of it. They just said because I hadn't applied myself, 'you just can't do that if you mess about the whole year'. Yeah well I was in the bottom set for everything, always in the naughty class or whatever. No one really taught anyone. The teachers would just sit back there and basically give up because everyone would ... it was all just the naughty kids, basically unteachable in a way, but I ended up doing alright. I got A–Cs. I could have got higher but you can't really get out [of the bottom set] ... the teachers would've given up, they just give you books and stuff, but ... I wasn't always in the bottom set; it was kind of slowly went down. So once you're in the high set and don't apply yourself same as the other kids, or you don't do the work, they will just drop you down the sets. So it's not on your results, it's on your application. It's dead end ... it's the write-off class, the bottom one. So I think the way they look at it is, they've taken out all the naughty kids out of all the other classes who distract all the other kids, they've shoved them all in one class so all the other kids can get the 80 per cent, 90 per cent.

(David)

This account makes for sobering reading and it is not the only such experience recounted to me by the participants.

This book explores some of the less constructive experiences as well as the more positive accounts of 15 young men who present their views about both the school and university systems in England today. It also offers practical suggestions that schools and teachers can implement in the classroom.

Theoretical frameworks and definitions

In this section, as well as reviewing the definitions and theoretical concepts that frame my work, I detail my motivations for exploring the educational experiences of academically successful white working-class young men and I begin with an exploration of the concept of class.

Class

Class and its relationship to educational inequality is pivotal to my study, but it is also a problematic notion as it is a highly contested concept. In the past, social class has been linked to occupational status and many researchers still use the Office for National Statistics' (ONS) National

Statistics Socio-economic Classification (NS-SEC) as their main tool for classifying the population's class. Recently, some sociologists have argued that 'this occupationally based class schema does not effectively capture the role of social and cultural processes in generating class divisions' (Savage *et al.*, 2013: 220). In consequence, there is sometimes a tension between seeing social class as a structural and material phenomenon related to occupational status and earnings and in taking it as a cultural formation. For example, how would we class-categorize a highly qualified theologian who earns a meagre stipend?

Class is a complicated construct made even more slippery in the sense of whether it is understood objectively (in terms of status/income) or subjectively (in terms of how people self-recognize or feel) or some combination of both. There are also class/ethnic differences, as is the case for some families who move to the UK from other parts of the world and occupy a working-class position but hold middle-class aspirations due to their origins and backgrounds. The white working classes themselves may be internally differentiated too, so that a community in rural working-class Norfolk may be very different from those living on an urban working-class council estate (Maguire, 2005).

These complications considered, in this book I take class to be intimately related to income/status as well as the self-perceptions of the young men who all self-identified as coming from a working-class background. The reasons given by the young men for so categorizing themselves included their parents' occupations, the level of their parents' academic qualifications and income, where they lived, and the schools they had attended. When asked about any welfare support they and their families had received, ten said they had been entitled to FSMs, ten had received the Educational Maintenance Allowance (EMA) in the sixth form, and 14 received maintenance grants at university. When I checked their Acorn UK postcode categories (CACI, 2014), I found that three of the young men's families lived in the lowest category (5), classified as 'Urban Adversity'; seven lived in category 4, described as 'Financially Stretched'; and the others lived in category 3, described as 'Comfortable Communities', or above.

While all of the participants may have described themselves as working class, they appeared to come from different *fractions* of the working class and this can be seen in Table 1.1, which shows the postcode categories from which they came. As Reay suggests, 'class makes a difference not just in terms of inter-class differences but also in terms of intra-class difference'

(1998b: 522), and it is the degree of economic hardship and poverty that differentiates these fractions of class (Maguire, 1997).

Table 1.1: Acorn UK postcode categories

Category	Number of participants
5 – Urban Adversity	3
4 – Financially Stretched	7
3 – Comfortable Communities	3
2 – Rising Prosperity	2

In addition to economic disparities, there can also be in-group differences between people of the same broad socio-economic group, related to their capacity to access various '*capitals*' (Bourdieu, 1990a), as illustrated by this quote from Leon, whose family home was in category 5:

> Although my family are working class technically, in terms of their interest and culture, they are not what you typically associate with working-class people. And I kind of think that culturally we are probably middle class.

Previous studies (Ball *et al.*, 2002; Jackson and Marsden, 1966) suggest that many working-class students who access higher education come from what they call the 'upper echelons' of the working class. However, being in the lowest (Acorn) category did not prevent two of the participants completing undergraduate degrees at elite universities and one completing his undergraduate studies at a modern university. Thus, class categorizations may be more complex than they appear; class-inflected research needs to take account of the subtle intra-class differences that exist as well as the broader inter-class differences.

Habitus, field, and capital

It seemed to me that in analysing factors to do with family circumstances, educational choice-making, and cultural patterns, Bourdieu's conceptual toolkit was highly applicable. His work offered a lens through which I could begin to tease out and explain those factors that enabled the young men to experience academic success. His approach lent me a distinctive way in which to frame my work; it provided me with a language and a conceptual array from which to work.

Bourdieu's work is best known for its focus on social class reproduction. He argued that habitus – that is, dispositions to choose and behave in certain ways, which are established in childhood – becomes a system of 'durable, transposable dispositions' that shape the choices people make and influence their ways of being (Bourdieu, 1990b: 53).

Bourdieu (1997) maintains that habitus is structured by one's family upbringing and life experiences and that cultural capital is transmitted within the family. Cultural capital becomes objectified as habitus and it is then realized and embodied in practice. These interactions and events occur in a social space that Bourdieu terms 'field'. He also argues that society is divided into different spheres or fields, such as politics and education, and that as individuals move into different fields they are more or less able to invest in these according to the capitals they have at their disposal.

Bourdieu produced an equation that shows how capitals become embodied as part of one's habitus and together with one's social field results in practice:

$$[(\text{habitus})(\text{capital})] + \text{field} = \text{practice (Bourdieu, 1984: 101)}.$$

The equation illuminates the interconnectedness of habitus, culture, and field; according to Bourdieu, these concepts work together to perpetuate the process of social class reproduction. Bourdieu claimed that because different forms of capital were and are in play, they can be used to access advantage in some cases. For example, in his theoretical framework, the middle classes know how the educational system works and inculcate in their children sets of values and practices that promote not only educational success but also occupational success. The corollary is that working-class families have access to different forms of cultural, social, and economic capital and therefore the educational decisions they make will be different. A practical example of this is apparent in the higher education sector, where the top rung of universities are inhabited mainly by middle-class students and post-1992 universities attract those from a working-class background (Sutton Trust, 2011).

Bourdieu's work proved very useful in mapping out the factors involved in the participants' experiences, such as shifts in their primary habitus and the role of field. However, the account I present is not one of straightforward social reproduction. My findings suggest there are several key factors that together contributed to the academic success of the young men and these are explored in Chapters 3 to 6.

Methodology and methods

My research concern was centred around the *individual* and understanding how the individual interprets their social world (Bryman, 2012). My aim was to gain some understanding of the factors that had been significant in the academic pathway of the participants and thus I chose a qualitative approach.

The method

As I wanted to learn about the participants' own accounts of how they had been academically successful, I chose semi-structured interviews as my research method. I believed that this form of interview would offer the young men an opportunity to expand on any issues that were raised and perhaps bring up factors I had not anticipated. I interviewed the young men three times over a two-year period: once at the beginning of their second year of university, again at the end of their second year, and then finally as they were leaving university. Interviewing the participants this number of times, over an extended period, meant that the young men became familiar and relaxed with me, and while they were very willing participants in the first interview, they appeared to be even more open in the second and third interviews. These latter interviews went on for extended periods of time, with much meaningful data coming to light.

Research questions

Based on my research interests, I formulated the following questions:

- How do academically successful white working-class young men account for their achievements?
- In what ways do academically successful white working-class young men interpret their university experiences?
- What reasons (if any) do academically successful white working-class males give for the under-achievement of many of their peers? What do they think could make an educational difference?

My sample

Recruiting for my study proved problematic. I had initially tried to recruit academically successful white working-class young men at the beginning of their second year of undergraduate study from one modern and one elite university via a circular email distributed at each institution. I received very few responses and therefore had to widen my net to encompass several more universities. After actively recruiting for a period of some months across several universities, 15 young men had consented to be part of my study. My initial aim was to recruit at least 20 participants; however, I moved forward with the young men I had. In the circular email I had posted at the various universities, I invited white working-class male undergraduates to participate in a research project and thus, in agreeing to take part, they had all 'self-identified' as coming from working-class families.

Representing the participants

By the time I completed my interviews, I had collected a large amount of data, and in selecting excerpts of data from this sea of information I understood that I, as the researcher-writer, had the power to represent the participants. I constantly reflected on my motives for carrying out the study and for using the data I chose to use. Although I recognized that I would benefit from the research, my main aim was to give voice to the young men who had willingly come forward to be interviewed and allow them to tell their stories of success. The principles I adhered to were those that Kvale (1996) suggests a researcher should live up to: honesty, justice, and respect for the person.

Data analysis

Based on my knowledge of the related research and my theoretical framework, I undertook an 'inductive' thematic content analysis of my data set involving iterative processes.

The first interview focused on the habitus and forms of capital (Bourdieu, 1984) these young men experienced in their homes, the impacts of the fields of primary and secondary schooling, and, in some cases, the sixth-form college they attended. The second interview focused on how they negotiated their way through their first two years of university. In the final interview, I explored their experiences during what was for most of them their final year of undergraduate study. I also explored the explanations they offered for the academic under-achievement of many of the white working-class boys they were at school with and their understandings of why this under-achievement was so prevalent among their friends.

The major themes that emerged from my coding and analysis of the initial interviews were: family, schooling, mentors, fractions of class, and misrecognition. Some of these codes were descriptive in style; others were more conceptual. The themes that emerged from the second interviews clustered around the commonalities and differences experienced at university by the young men. Here the themes tended to be more descriptive. The final interviews dealt with the sense of disengagement with education experienced by many young white working-class men. Emergent themes included: family, schools and teachers, mentors, lack of aspiration, and fear of failure. The data obtained from the three interviews and the themes that emerged from the data analysis form the basis of Chapters 3 to 6.

Outline of the book
Chapter 2: Higher education for all?
In England, one of the most dramatic shifts in education in the latter half of the twentieth century and into the twenty-first century has been the expansion of higher education. In the late nineteenth century less than 1 per cent of young people were in higher education, and even in the late 1950s only 3 per cent of the population attended university (Wolf, 2002). However, by 1997 there was a 30 per cent participation rate in higher education and the latest UCAS figures show that by age 19, nearly 50 per cent of all young people in England are in higher education, yet the rate for white young men on FSMs is less than 10 per cent (UCAS, 2016).

This chapter brings together a set of interrelated aspects of higher education and considers how they relate to working-class attendance at university. The Bourdieusian concepts of habitus, field, and capital are used to conceptualize this relationship. The diverse environments in different 'types' of university are examined, as well as the question of how working-class students choose the type of higher education institution to attend. Their expectations and transitions to, and experiences of, higher education are explored. Specifically, white working-class young men's access to higher education is analysed and this chapter provides a backdrop to the exploration of the university experiences of the participants. The chapter's fundamental argument is that educational success has been and still is highly atypical for white working-class males and that those who do achieve do so *despite* the odds.

Chapter 3: Early life and schooling
Here I map out how my original 15 participants successfully negotiated the school system and obtained admittance to university, drawing on data obtained from the initial in-depth interviews undertaken when the young men were in the first term of their second year of university. The focus in this chapter is on the habitus and forms of capital these young men experienced in their families and the influence of the fields of the primary and secondary school they attended.

All 15 stories tell a tale of achievement *against the odds*. Persistence and sheer determination were needed by all of the participants at various stages in their schooling. All 15 had to manoeuvre their way through a system that was littered with obstacles, making their arrival at university all the more surprising. It is little wonder then that in the academic year 2011/12 (the year that they entered university), only 21 per cent of *all* young people on FSMs (not just white working-class young men on FSMs) entered university (DfE, 2016b).

Chapter 4: Experiences at university

This chapter explores how 14 of the original 15 young white men I recruited negotiated their way through the first two years of university, with a variety of key themes being identified as crucial to their academic achievement. The first year away from home can be difficult for all undergraduate students. It is also well documented that attending university can induce high levels of pressure and anxiety. However, by the second year, all bar one of the original participants had decided to continue with their studies and most were now settled into the new field of university life. It was evident from what they said that there had been changes in their linguistic codes as well as their cultural and social capital.

All but one of the participants had received maintenance grants, with seven of the remaining young men attending modern universities and seven attending elite universities.

Chapter 5: A degree ... what now?

The young men's perceptions of university life, the costs as well as the benefits of obtaining a degree, and any changes they and/or others may have noticed in themselves are explored and analysed in this chapter. The career ambitions of the young men are also examined. Those who had attended modern universities tended to go into fields such as football coaching, physical education (PE) teaching, or retail management. The young men with degrees from elite universities followed career paths that took them into the law, consulting, librarianship, IT, and PhD research. Data for this chapter is drawn from the analysis of the final set of in-depth interviews conducted when the young men were at the end of their third and, in many cases, final year of study.

Chapter 6: Why white working-class males do not engage academically

When I started my research, I set out to discover, from the perspectives of a group of young academically successful white working-class men, how it was that they had done well against the odds. In this chapter, I broaden my scope and examine the reasons these young men gave for the under-achievement of many of their peers. The participants' suggestions for steps that could make an educational difference to other white working-class boys are also explored.

Chapter 7: Conclusions: Drawing the study together

In this chapter, I revisit the intentions of my research and the thorny question of what is meant by the term 'working-class', and I summarize my key findings. I conclude with a discussion of some of the key policy implications that arise from my study and I argue that these are not only relevant for policymakers but also for teachers, teacher educators, university outreach programmers/co-ordinators, and university widening participation centres.

Chapter 8: Epilogue: Where are they now?

The possibility of an epilogue came to me as I wrote the book. I thought an update three years after the last interview could be insightful. The aim was to establish how the young men had adjusted to work, their thoughts on the benefits or otherwise of university some years after leaving, and an exploration of their ongoing relationships with family and friends.

I began by contacting the young men, with nine agreeing to be interviewed again, four providing sketchy updates via phone or electronically, and two failing to respond. The updates form the basis of this chapter.

To sum up

My study highlights the factors that contributed to the academic success of the young men and the hurdles they had to overcome to achieve this success. These young men worked hard at achieving their aims and for them it was a day-to-day and year-to-year commitment; they experienced disappointments, but they did not let these get in the way of their aim of successfully negotiating their way through the school system. Most had had the benefit of teachers who encouraged them academically and their experiences at school left them with positive learner identities. However, not all children develop positive learner identities and from what the participants said, there appear to be some in-school practices that act as dampeners on the academic aspirations of white working-class boys. The young men recounted that some of their teachers had little expectation that white working-class boys would experience academic success. Thus, it could be argued that the 'habitus' of the school positions (some) white working-class males as 'not academic' and this view underpins everything that takes place in the classroom.

What I hope that this book does, through drawing on the lived experiences and perceptions of a small number of white young men from working-class families, is raise the awareness of all those associated with educating white working-class young men of the consequences of labelling children. They need to understand the possible effect this can and does have on the aspirations of the students themselves, their parents, and teachers. Teachers should never underestimate the influence they have on children and need to remember that their comments, whether positive or negative, can remain with a child for ever.

Chapter 2

Higher education for all?

> ... *those students from poorer backgrounds who make it to university are likely to be intellectually as well as socially remarkable.*
>
> (Clegg, 2011: 95)

The massification of higher education in England

One of the most dramatic shifts in education in the UK since the early 1960s has been the expansion of higher education (HE). The number of universities has grown from just 22 universities in the early 1960s to over 150 in 2015 (Bathmaker *et al.*, 2016). Participation rates among the young (18–19 year olds) has increased from 3 per cent in the late 1950s to almost 50 per cent in 2013/14 (DfE, 2016a).

The widening participation policy, begun in 1963 with the publication of the Robbins Report and accelerated in the late 1990s by the then Labour Government, was set up for both economic and social reasons. On an economic level, the government anticipated that widening participation in HE would improve the economy at local, regional, and national levels, which would in turn make the country more competitive on a global level. It was also believed that the development of an individual's personal capabilities would boost his or her prosperity levels. On a social level, widening participation in HE was seen as a means by which disadvantaged social groups could achieve social mobility (Bathmaker *et al.*, 2016; DfES, 2003). The young men from a working-class background who agreed to participate in this research were very much part of the target group in this drive to widen the participation in HE. However, despite the growth in the numbers of young people attending higher education institutions (HEIs), this growth has not been evenly spread across the social classes, with only 22 per cent of pupils eligible for free school meals (FSMs) attending university (DfE, 2016b). Young people such as the participants remain very much a minority, despite the raft of policies implemented in recent decades by successive governments to target this group.

One powerful illustration of the socio-economic gap between university enrolment for FSM students and those who have been to independent schools is contained in Figure 2.1. Of the 78,179 pupils entitled to FSM in 2005/06, 1,414 (1.8 per cent) entered one of the top 30 universities in the UK, referred to here as 'the Sutton 30' (see Appendix 1), compared with 41 per cent of independently educated students.

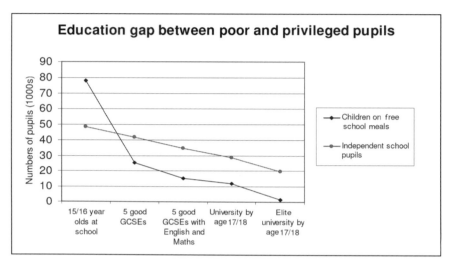

Figure 2.1: Education gap between poor and privileged students, 2005/06 to 2007/08
Source: Sutton Trust (2010: 13)

Figure 2.2 provides another powerful illustration of social class difference in HE attendance by comparing socio-economic status (SES), gender, and ethnicity. It reveals that only 10 per cent of young white working-class men on FSMs go to university; and of that 10 per cent, less than 1 per cent go to Oxford or Cambridge (Crawford and Greaves, 2015). So, while the massification of universities has led to a large increase in the number of young people attending, the socio-economic gap remains stubbornly large. This conundrum is explored in greater detail later in the book, as are the reasons why my respondents, all but one of whom were entitled to FSMs at some time in their school careers, managed to obtain entrance to university when most of their cohort did not.

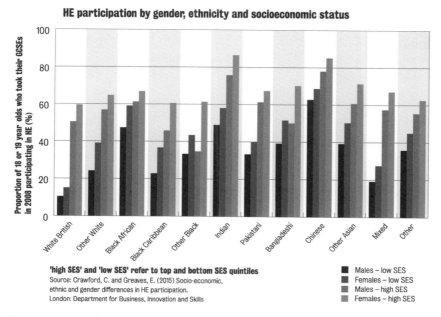

Figure 2.2: Higher education participation by gender, ethnicity, and socio-economic status

The intensification of the hierarchy of universities

The massification of universities has also led to a distinctive hierarchy and institutional diversity developing among the universities in England. This hierarchy is composed of: elite universities, which are the oldest universities in the country; red-brick universities, built in industrial towns in England at the beginning of the twentieth century; pre-1992 universities (those universities that were built after the Second World War); and post-1992 or modern universities, which were originally polytechnics or colleges of further education (FE). This institutional diversity reflects differences in such aspects as their culture, mission, size, subject mix, and proportion of residential to commuting students. This results in students having different university experiences depending on the classification of the university attended (Brennan and Osborne, 2008). This is explored in more detail later in the chapter.

Forms of capital and higher education choices

In Bourdieu's theoretical framework, the middle classes know *how* the educational system works:

> Those sections which are richest in cultural capital are more
> inclined to invest in their children's education at the same time
> as in cultural practices liable to maintain and increase their
> specific rarity.
>
> (Bourdieu, 1997: 502)

Devine (2004) also argues that middle-class parents inculcate a set of
values and practices that promotes not only educational success but also
occupational success for their children. The corollary is that working-class
families have access to different forms of cultural, social, and economic
capital and therefore the educational and occupational decisions they make
will be different.

In relation to choosing or selecting HEIs Bourdieu and Passeron
(1977) suggest that middle-class parents use their cultural capital to aid
their children in acquiring qualifications from elite universities or the
'best' ones they can access. Indeed, Brown asserts that education selection
is more often based on the 'wealth and wishes of parents rather than the
individual abilities and efforts of the pupils' and he goes on to suggest that
the equation 'ability + effort = merit' has been reformulated into 'resources
+ preference = choice' (Brown, 1995: 44). He does not see the increase in
the numbers attending university as an equalizing of opportunity. Rather,
he sees an increasing differential between the various universities and what
they offer their students.

Crawford *et al.* (2017) agree that the most highly selective
universities are attended mainly by middle-class students, and post-1992
universities mainly by those from a working-class background. The Sutton
Trust (2011) found that, over a three-year period from 2007 to 2009, 48
per cent of independent school students gained entry to the Sutton 30
highly selective universities, compared with only 18 per cent of students in
comprehensive schools.

As suggested earlier, universities differ from each other along
a range of dimensions, for instance: their location, including whether
students live in accommodation near the university or live at home; the
curriculum offered to students, and the flexibility and options offered; entry
requirements; and the populations they serve. Crozier *et al.* (2008) identify
a 'polarisation of types of university attracting working-class and minority
ethnic students' (p. 167) and suggest that students are exposed to different
experiences within the different types of university. These differences in turn
reflect a differentiation in wealth and organization of the various types of
university as well as their expectations of the students and the students'

individual socio-cultural backgrounds (Crozier *et al.*, 2008; see also Sutton Trust, 2000).

This means that, for the most part, working-class students attend less selective and lower-status universities. It has also been asserted that qualifications obtained from lower-status universities are considered to hold less exchange value in the labour market than those from the more selective universities attended by many middle-class students (Brown, 2013; Crawford *et al.*, 2017).

Devine (2004) claims that middle-class parents have the expectation that their children will succeed academically because they *know* that their children are academically able and they also *know* what their children need to do to succeed. She argues that working-class parents on the other hand may also aspire for their children to be academically successful but they do not tend to have the same confidence. Their occupational expectations for their children also differ from middle-class parents and they are 'happy' to see their children in any occupation that is seen as an improvement on their own blue-collar employment and status.

Students from a working-class background who aspire to further their academic careers can be faced with 'difficult choices and limited resources'. Some of these choices are economic in nature: for instance, they may have to weigh up the opportunity costs of remaining outside the labour force for an extended period and the concept of a delayed payoff may be beyond their own and their family's economic capability (Devine, 2004). In England, this opportunity cost has become even more relevant since September 2012, when university tuition fees rose to £9,000 per year, though to date this rise in fees does not appear to have deterred students from a working-class background from applying to university (Crawford *et al.*, 2017).

Officially, the ability to participate in HE is portrayed 'in meritocratic and individual terms, but in reality, the actual costs and benefits of participation are unevenly socially structured' (Clegg, 2011: 95). Middle-class students, not faced with the same economic, cultural, or social restrictions faced by working-class students, attend universities that allow them to build up their cultural and social capital. Reay *et al.* (2005) see 'choice' as being intrinsically linked with the cultural capital and the habitus of the student. Their research found that middle-class students see moving to HE as a natural, orderly, and clear-cut process whereas working-class students experience educational choice as a risky and constrained process.

Many middle-class students 'know' that it is in their best interests to attend university and they are encouraged and supported by their parents, who have the relevant cultural as well as the economic capital to ensure that their children not only go to university but go to what they perceive as a *good* university. Once at these universities, middle-class students can consolidate and enhance their cultural and social capital (Dorling, 2014; Sutton Trust, 2013).

In their endeavour for academic excellence and credentialization, students from a working-class background must go through the daunting process of obtaining entrance to university. But, even before this, achieving the GCSE grades that enable them to continue with their studies is a *major* hurdle for many working-class students (Dilnot, 2016). Once this hurdle has been overcome, they need to navigate their way through the sixth form. As the first in their families to stay on at school beyond the compulsory leaving age, many students from a working-class background – such as the participants – find choosing subjects that enable them to attend university a stressful experience. Most have no prior family knowledge of A levels or of university entrance requirements. Some of the study participants spent three years in the sixth form in their efforts to obtain the necessary qualifications to go on to higher education and the advice given by schools and FE institutions can be vitally important in the HE choosing process. Schools are an important source of knowledge for students who have no family history of further or higher education.

The impact of schools and further education colleges on university choice

Research has shown that different types of school affect their students' choices of post-compulsory schooling, with most students attending schools with a sixth form aspiring to attend university. This was the case for both higher and lower socio-economic status (SES) schools; although with 85 per cent of their students favouring university, the higher SES schools were slightly ahead of those schools with the lower SES catchment, which had 74 per cent favouring university (Foskett *et al.*, 2008).

This finding contrasted with those schools without a sixth form, where the majority of students expressed a desire to pursue vocational courses. Schools in low SES areas reported that 79 per cent of their students wanted to do vocational courses while schools in higher SES areas had 68 per cent of their students expressing an interest in pursuing vocational courses. Foskett *et al.* concluded that schools and sixth-form colleges 'control' and 'manage' students' choices and decisions in different ways.

Ball *et al.* (2002) also found that the HEI chosen by students was related to the school they attended. They saw 'school effect' as an independent variable and described it as 'institutional habitus'. Expectations of choice were constructed over time, based on the views and advice of teachers and fellow students and the learning experience, with a clear relationship between the 'family habituses and the institutional habituses' (Ball *et al.*, 2002: 58).

While students' HE choices are influenced by family, friends, and educational institution attended, and their own perceptions and beliefs, there are, according to Reay *et al.*, specific effects from attending a particular educational institution (2005). A joint report by BIS (Department for Business, Innovation and Skills) and Sutton Trust (2009) found that the number of university applications from FE colleges to the Sutton 30 group of universities (see Appendix 1 for a list) was less than half that of other types of school. This applied even after accounting for the differences in average overall levels of A level attainment of the schools and colleges. They found that students from FE colleges were less likely than students from schools with a sixth form to choose to study at the most selective universities, even on achieving the prerequisite A level results (BIS and Sutton Trust, 2009).

Five of the 15 young men went to FE colleges, of whom four went to modern universities. Reay *et al.* (2005) suggest several possible reasons why this might be the case. These include differences in *careers advice* received, or in some cases the lack of careers advice received, and the *curriculum offered* at the different educational institutions. For example, studying 'new' subjects such as media studies in the sixth form can limit university choice as 'elite' and 'red-brick' universities usually require 'traditional' subjects, whereas post-1992 universities are open to accepting students who have studied the newer subjects. The *level of advice* about university choice in FE colleges is also often limited, and the relationship between the specific knowledge the individual student has about HEIs and the *parameters the school sets* around which HEIs their students should apply to combine to limit the student's choices (Reay *et al.*, 2005).

Students' own expectations and experiences of higher education

As has been suggested, each university has its own 'institutional habitus' and students are acutely aware of this. Applicants to HE from a working-class background are very concerned with 'fitting in' and 'feeling comfortable' with the university. This often results in them seeing the elite universities as 'not for the likes of us' because they feel that the institutional habitus alienates or 'others' them. The priority for many working-class students is to go to a university where they feel comfortable and where they may 'feel at home within education' (Crozier *et al.*, 2008). Working-class students tend to be attracted to post-1992 universities because they offer more open access and encourage diverse applicants. This is borne out by the results of a study conducted by BIS and Sutton Trust (2009) that analysed the destination universities of a cohort of students. Of the cohort, 300,000 were working-class students and just over 1 per cent of them went to the Sutton 30 universities (see Appendix 1).

Having made the transition to university, the first-generation HE students then enter a milieu with which they are unfamiliar (Crozier *et al.*, 2008). They find themselves accessing a field that does not match their habitus and where there are new rules of the game (Bourdieu, 1990b). University can be a fraught experience, at least initially, for first-generation university students who lack the appropriate cultural capital. They need to find ways to engage with this new environment.

The Reay *et al.* (2005) study on the HE choices of working-class students found that the transition to HE for these students could be complex and difficult. They struggled with many issues that middle-class students did not have to consider. Two-thirds of the working-class school students in the study were in some type of paid employment, which resulted in them having less time available for study. Working-class students are also often confined in their choice of university by geography. Many are committed to living in a specific locality for reasons such as family or work commitments, and for economic reasons such as the cost of travel and accommodation. The only time these students spent at university was time spent in classes, as most of them worked. Students living at home often continue with the same work patterns, leisure activities, and social networks that they employed while at school (Hayton and Paczuska, 2002). Conversely, according to Reay *et al.* (2010), working-class students who attend pre-1992 universities appeared to embrace university life and to have a stronger sense of themselves as university students than those who attended post-1992 universities. These students were, however, also very aware of being in a predominantly middle-class institution – in other words 'like a fish out of water' (Bourdieu and Wacquant, 1992).

Chapters 4 and 5 examine these issues in relation to the choices made by the participants.

Working-class students and withdrawal rates

In England, the withdrawal rate among working-class students is much higher than in those from middle-class backgrounds. Additionally, withdrawal rates among universities vary enormously, with elite and red-brick universities having much lower withdrawal rates than the post-1992 universities.

Research consistently shows that working-class students are more likely to attend post-1992 universities as they have been the most successful at widening participation, but they also have the highest withdrawal rates, with the figures for 2009/10 showing that more than one in five undergraduates failed to complete the first year of their degree course at the lower-performing universities. To take the example of withdrawal rates at two different types of university: the withdrawal rate for the University of Cambridge for 2009/10 was 0.6 per cent whereas for the University of Bolton it was 21 per cent (HESA, 2013). Could this be because the students at modern universities are, as Reay *et al.* (2010) suggest, not as committed as those students who attend pre-1992 and elite universities? Could their outside commitments mean they cannot devote the necessary time to their studies? All of the young men in the study who had attended elite universities completed their studies, whereas two of the attendees at modern universities withdrew in their second year. This speaks to the withdrawal rates examined and is explored further in Chapter 4.

In their study of provincial young white working-class men who did initially go to, and then withdrew from, post-1992 universities, Quinn *et al.* (2006) found that withdrawing 'was a rational decision' (p. 746). For all of these young men, money was an ever-present problem and there were other reasons such as the timing not being right, the subject not meeting expectations, or circumstances in general not being conducive to attending university. 'They had to learn to live with poverty and debt as a normalised part of everyday life' (Quinn *et al.*, 2006: 744). Hutchings and Archer (2001) also found that poverty and debt were seen as inevitable side effects of going to university for the working-class applicants in their study. As such, it acted as a major deterrent.

Working-class students find themselves in riskier positions than their middle-class counterparts and therefore have fewer participation choices. Their HE choices are not only limited by their educational achievements but also by their concerns regarding their financial position, family situation, loss of working-class identity, disadvantage within the HE system, chances of failure, and their ability to find work on completion of their study (Archer and Hutchings, 2000). While I have been unable to follow up with the young men who withdrew from university and therefore could not establish their reasons for withdrawing, I do know that they both worked while at university and one of them was working full time. As Skeggs (1997) states: 'To think that class does not matter is only a prerogative of those unaffected by the deprivations and exclusions it produces' (p. 7).

White working-class access to higher education

The gender balance in HE has changed dramatically. In 1960, just under 4 per cent of the population went to university, with young women making up less than 20 per cent of the cohort. Women now make up 56.4 per cent of the entire student population. It has also emerged that white working-class men are the least likely of any group to enter HE and, along with black African-Caribbean men, are the most disengaged from HE. This has resulted in more young women from poorer backgrounds progressing to HE than young men from the same background (Equality Challenge Unit, 2013).

It has been suggested that young working-class men are more attracted to the world of work after compulsory schooling than to the world of further and higher education. Some researchers argue that for young working-class men, their masculinity (habitus) does not necessarily fit comfortably with the world of education, much less higher education (Cleary, 2007; Connell, 1989; Willis, 1977). Many young working-class men see education as 'feminine' and therefore, once again, 'not for the likes of me' (Archer and Yamashita, 2003). Cleary (2007) in her study, which focused on issues of male and female participation rates in FE in the west of Scotland, found that the young white working-class men in her study were motivated to find full-time work and establish a family. Their aspirations were associated with working hard, having an income, and enjoying themselves at the end of the week. Many working-class young men had not enjoyed their schooling experience and this seemed to affect their decisions about HE; they were not motivated to attain more educational qualifications and there were clear social expectations for men to take up traditionally male jobs.

Concluding remarks

Not everyone enters the HE market with the same levels of cultural or educational capital and, while there has been a substantial growth in the number of universities since 1963, the research suggests that students from a working-class background who do make it to university predominantly choose 'modern' universities. However, as the figures show, even the modern universities have been only moderately successful at widening participation, with just 22 per cent of students on FSMs attending any university (DfE, 2016b). These findings form the backdrop to my own research and lead me to the next chapter, in which I examine the early life and schooling of the 15 young men who bucked the trend.

Chapter 3
Early life and schooling

If you, as an individual, give a child the belief that they can achieve anything they want to, they often will. Not just in the classroom, but in life.

(Wigdortz, 2012)

The focus in this chapter is on the data obtained in the first interview, which centres on the family lives of these young men, their school experiences, and the complex processes they went through to obtain admission to university. The myriad data collected means that I cannot do justice to each participant's complex family and schooling history, so the individual quotes extracted from the interviews and used throughout the remainder of the book were selected as illustrative and representative examples. They clarify the emergent themes identified as significant from the young men's accounts and the literature. Appendix 2 offers a brief biographical description of each of the participants.

Emergent themes
I began the first interview by asking the young men about their family backgrounds and what became immediately obvious was the role their mothers played in providing constant support for them during their educational trajectory.

Another key emergent theme centred around schooling. Most of the participants experienced academic success early in their lives and only one of the interviewees had negative feelings about his primary school years. However, there were divergent experiences at secondary level. The emergent themes are divided into subsections and are more fully explored below.

Mother matters
In their classic study, undertaken in the early 1960s, on working-class families whose children went on to grammar school, Jackson and Marsden (1966) found 'that the centres of power usually lay with the mother' (p. 97). This pattern emerged with my sample. Mark explained that 'my mum actually put our house up for sale because she wanted us to live in the catchment area' of a good secondary school. Harvey recounted that his mother was the instigator of them visiting universities. 'This was all my

mum's doing, my dad and I were like, "do we have to go?".' He also recalled that 'my dad just sort of like sat back and let my mum take control of me'. 'She tries to influence me in *everything*,' Nathan told me when talking about his mother.

Reay (2005) also found that in educational matters it was the mothers who exercised most influence. The mothers of the participants appeared to have the cultural capital necessary to encourage their sons to pursue higher education, and it was they who consistently emphasized its importance. Karl recalled his mother saying: 'You do well in education you will be able to succeed ... get a good education, go to university, and it should all be good.' Oliver recalled that his mother would not let him go out after school: 'You are not leaving, you are doing the revision.'

The respondents emphasized their parents' desires for them to have better lives than they did. Nathan, whose father was a bricklayer, recounted: 'My dad said you don't want to be stacking shelves in Somerfield for a living.' Leon explained that he and his mother never had much money and that his mother made him aware that a good education would give him the opportunity of 'having enough money so you don't struggle and having a life that enables you to explore what you're interested in'. The parents saw education as the means by which their sons could improve their economic situation through the process of completing a higher education degree.

One of my participants, John, informed me that his parents had been 'underestimated when they were kids. I think they let that get to them and they didn't realize how good they were.' Because they themselves had these negative academic experiences as youngsters, John's parents actively encouraged him to achieve. Oliver reported that his mother had told him: 'Your strength is your brain not your hands, so I was like fair enough.' Most of the participants were strongly encouraged to study. The families believed that higher education would enable economic success (Hutchings and Archer, 2001). The young men seemed bound into a culture of escape and bettering themselves. The habitus of the home, and the cultural values that their parents held, instilled in their sons the benefits of higher education.

Most of them recalled their mothers or fathers reading to them and encouraging them to read and most claimed they could read before they started formal school. Leon said: 'I was taught to read before I went to school and always enjoyed reading.' Ben recalled that it was his father who read to him when he was a toddler. 'My dad used to sit me down with picture books and kind of say what this is and what's that?' John also recalled that his father 'helped me extend myself ... when I was younger we'd like sit on the carpet and he would make us do our tables and stuff'.

This involvement of the father was unusual as most participants told me that it was their mother who insisted on them doing their homework. Harvey commented: 'They [the other boys] were out playing football and I had to come home and do my homework.' Discipline was mentioned by many of the participants. Adam told me: 'I was always forced to behave.' Others mentioned a nurturing family environment. Leon said: 'It has just basically been a very interesting environment to grow up in.' Adam told me: 'My parents were always very supportive.'

Most of the participants reported that their mothers did not feel adequately educated to help their sons academically once they entered secondary school. As Reay (1998a) found in her study on mothers, while working-class mothers were engaged in the educational processes their children were going through, they generally had fewer cultural and economic resources, fewer educational qualifications, and less knowledge about the education system than middle-class mothers. For these reasons, they felt less able to help their children with their education as the children progressed into secondary school. Their role while passive was supportive; they were there to support their children through the education process. As Craig recalled: 'She [his mother] had the most profound effect on my academics because she would always listen even if she didn't understand.'

The participants' mothers were all in employment, as Appendix 3 shows, and it is possible that some of them have improved their cultural knowledge through their employment, experiencing what Savage (2000) refers to as 'different cultural styles' (p. 117). Four of the mothers work in education, and perhaps working in schools has increased their knowledge of what education options are available. Karl's mother was a childminder and her charges were a teacher's children. Karl stated that it was this teacher who had informed his mother of how best he could get into university when he did not do as well as expected in his A levels. The mothers constantly instilled in their sons a notion of 'bettering yourself' (Archer and Hutchings, 2000).

Parental aspiration and higher education

The respondents all spoke positively about their parents' aspirations for them. Ben recalled that his parents encouraged him to sit his 11-plus exams and go to grammar school, as well as encouraging him to apply to university. Adam explained that he was encouraged to do well academically: 'I was always told I should try my best as I was wasting opportunities if I wasn't.'

As Leon explained: 'My mum has always been, really valued education and knew that I was bright and that I could do well if I wanted to … she feels now that she made the wrong choice in terms of her career earnings.' Leon was brought up by his mother; he never knew his father. He also explained that he saw his grandmother and uncle as part of his immediate family. While they did not live in the same house, they did live very close by and had been actively involved in Leon's upbringing. Leon's aunt had done medicine at an elite university and it appears as if the habitus in which Leon grew up was one in which he was exposed to the economic benefits of a good education.

Interestingly, several of the parents themselves had gone on to higher education later in life. David informed me that his mother had 'recently, about five years ago, she did like a degree to like further enhance her nursing skills'. John recounted how his father was made redundant in 2007 and decided to attend university to do a maths and education degree. In the process, their mentoring role was reversed:

> I have been helping him out with his university course rather than [him] helping me out. He's quite demanding in that respect, you know you help him once, you will help him through his entire degree course for the whole three years!

The alleged lack of parental aspiration for their children's education has often been cited as a barrier to working-class educational achievement (DCSF, 2010) and one could suggest that it was because my respondents' parents had positive aspirations for their sons that these young men experienced academic success. However, they were often the only sibling in the family to attend university. In three families, younger siblings were undecided about their academic futures, and 11 of the participants' 19 siblings had/have no plans to access higher education. Thus, it can be seen from these examples that going to university is not a given in these families. Although my participants have successfully navigated their way through the school system and attended university, most of their siblings did not or do not necessarily plan to do so.

This raises the question of what is it in the habitus of the young men that led them to achieve academically while in many cases their siblings did not? Needless to say, this is a somewhat complex matter as it problematizes the concept of habitus. Perhaps this reflects the 'individualization' that Savage suggests is possible within Bourdieu's concepts of culture and habitus. A person can acquire the necessary cultural values and cultural capital to perform well in the education system, which in turn allows them to transform their individual habitus (Savage, 2000).

Mentor

Mentoring was important for the academic success of all the young men. Most of them could recall a teacher who mentored them and sometimes a 'meaningful other' who fulfilled that role. Frank described his older brother as his hero: 'When I needed a dad and needed someone to look up to … he was always more than happy to help.' This brother 'helped' in an emotional way, offering advice and practical support. Frank recalls, when he learned that he had been offered a place at university, his brother telling him 'how proud he was of me'.

Craig described how his mother 'was very, very, supportive all the way through and has encouraged me to do the best I can at school'. It was, however, only when his mother met a new partner that Craig realized that he could do much better. Craig recounted: 'So when Jim came along he was, "you know you are clever, you should try and do what you want to".' Mentors can help young people set and realize personally relevant goals. Mentors can also raise aspirations, providing access to a different kind of social and cultural capital (Ramaswami and Dreher, 2007). With his aspirations raised, Craig went on to study at an elite university.

Some respondents had teacher mentors in both primary and secondary school, while for others it was at one or the other. Harvey recalls having a mentor in both primary and secondary school. In Year 5 he recounted how 'I was quite good at maths so she [the Year 5 teacher] sort of like said, would you like to come and do this after school and stuff, so I just sort of done that.' He was in the gifted and talented programme for maths in secondary school. He explained that 'our maths teacher was head of it [the gifted and talented programme], so that is how I got into it'. Craig recalled a teacher at secondary school who would come in on a Saturday morning to give him extra lessons. 'She was fundamental in allowing me to realize that I could go far … I remember her saying I was just like a sponge.'

Ian, who did maths and computer science at an elite university, recalled his maths GCSE teacher providing him with extra learning opportunities. He recounts that his teacher said to him: '"I can start teaching you some calculus" and so he just kind of, he encouraged us to go further forward instead of just doing the work we kind of easily could do and stopping there.'

Mentoring can expose those being mentored to educational opportunities that motivate them to seek out new experiences and enhance their social and cultural capital (Spencer, 2007). John recalled with affection his politics teacher, at the sixth-form college, who convinced him to apply to an elite university. This teacher took some of the students to visit two elite universities. 'Which is why I applied here [the university he studied at] and he was very helpful, and, sometimes he brings me back to the [sixth-form] college to speak to the kids there who are dying to ask me questions.'

Mentors or meaningful others can help those they are mentoring to raise their aspirations:

> The teachers I had for English and history were very, very strong and they basically, they discussed university a lot more with you and really tried to improve our work and get you to degree standard.
>
> (Leon, who studied English at an elite university)

Only one young man, Edward, claimed to have had no teacher mentor. The other 14 all recalled at least one teacher who had provided academic stimulus, support, and guidance as well as non-academic support. Frank recalled his tutor in Years 10 and 11 saying to him '[you] look you are heading the same path as your brother, stop it'. Frank went on:

> I was just like 'oh' because my brother mucked about so he didn't really go into Year 11 ... he [the teacher] said it would be a waste if I just kept mucking about and it made me realize, yes I need to get on.

Frank's teacher mentor was acting in a paternalistic and 'intense' manner (Jacobi, 1991). His wake-up call jolted Frank into the realization that if he wanted to achieve his ambition of being a teacher he had to change his behaviour. When the young men spoke about their teacher mentors it was always in positive terms.

The teacher mentors had access to 'middle-class' cultural and social capital. They also modelled the usefulness of academic study, being pro-school, and having aspirations to attend university – values that may not always sit well with some versions of masculinity that challenge these values. These teacher mentors used their capital to encourage the young men to develop their own cultural and social capitals, achieve academically, and mobilize their positions in social space. According to Bourdieu (1984), each class occupies a position in social space that over time has been shaped and formed by the members within it. Each class has its own habitus and cultural capital and the individuals within it understand their place in society and what is and is not available to them. The young men have mobilized themselves with the help of mentors.

The primary school years

Most of the participants went to their local primary school (see Appendix 4), but three sets of parents actively chose schools. Mark's parents had two primary schools to choose from in their local catchment area and they chose the one they did because, as Mark recounted: 'Mum knew a teacher and she had given her loads of positive reviews so that was that!' Nathan's mother had to drive him to school because it was quite a distance from home. Nathan recalled that: 'There were two or three closer [schools] than the one I went to ... It was a C of E [Church of England].' John's mother sent him to the Roman Catholic primary school, which was also some distance from their home. It appears that these parents had been able to access what is considered middle-class knowledge and beliefs – the cultural and social capital to understand that not all schools are equal (Bourdieu, 1984) and that their sons would potentially benefit academically from attending certain schools instead of others.

The young men reported mixed experiences at primary school and, though most felt that they did achieve academic success early on, some recounted that their time in the primary school years was not enjoyable. Graham told me that: 'I didn't really enjoy school much in primary school because there wasn't any motivational figure or anything.' He went on to explain: 'The stuff we were doing in primary school was really, really basic and not particularly interesting.' While he experienced academic success, he did not enjoy the experience. On the other hand, Oliver had very fond memories of primary school: 'It was fantastic, absolutely fantastic. Lovely teachers, lovely staff, lovely setting, beautiful facilities.' Ian recalled that in primary school: 'I think I was pretty aware that I was brighter than the rest of them.'

Two of the young men mentioned that they had had special needs and this caused them some problems at primary school. David recalled: 'I was quite disruptive I think. I have, like dyslexia and I think struggled quite a lot with learning and didn't really understand, so I got moved quite a lot, from about three primary schools.' Leon also experienced problems:

> I received a diagnosis of Asperger's syndrome and ADHD [attention deficit hyperactivity disorder] when I was about ten but before that I tended sort of to have temper tantrums and be quite argumentative and hyperactive and not really know why and get into trouble for that and that meant I often found it hard to sort of have and maintain relationships with other people and teachers.

He went on to reveal that once he had been diagnosed:

> It made it easier for me to understand why I would often feel what I did and also it made it easier for my family ... this was just before I went to secondary school so it felt like a new start and I was able to start that off positively.

The diagnoses were a release for Leon as it enabled him, his family, and his teachers to understand that his problems were due to having Asperger's syndrome (and ADHD), not bad behaviour, and, as he said, he had the opportunity for a 'new start'. Leon's mother, who is a teaching assistant, perhaps understood the educational value of getting her son diagnosed through her ability to access the appropriate cultural capital; perhaps she was aware that once her son was diagnosed he would receive extra provisions at school and that his 'bad' behaviour would be seen in a different light. Leon's diagnosis made a difference to his self-perception and others' perceptions of him. It also changed his academic trajectory.

Secondary school

All but one participant experienced academic success at primary school and moved on positively to secondary school. One young man attended an all-boys grammar school. Three of them went on to secondary church schools and the remainder attended their local secondary schools.

Once again, some parents seemed to be aware that not all schools are the same and made concerted efforts to ensure that their sons attended secondary schools that they saw as *academically better*. These parents appear to have had the cultural capital necessary to see this process through (Bourdieu, 1984).

While not all families actively chose the secondary school their son attended, they all appeared to value and encourage learning. Adam explained that his parents emphasized the need 'to try our best and to take every opportunity, not just because our parents wanted us to do well but they wanted us to have the best chances'. Harvey recalled: 'My mum always like wanted me to do well. So she always pushed me in the right directions ... like it was mainly her idea to come to uni.'

Only one of the young men, Ben, went to a selective school from Year 7 through to Year 13. Ben explained that there were two selective all-boys grammar schools in his area as well as comprehensive schools and he visited them all first with his parents. Ben recalled that his parents encouraged him to go to one of the grammar schools and:

I kind of assumed you would probably do better if you went to like, in your qualifications, if you went to a grammar school because the grades are higher, I wasn't blind to that.

Ben also recalled that in Year 6 his teacher actively encouraged some of the children in his class to apply to grammar school: 'We were encouraged to do that … we did practice tests at school and we were encouraged in that respect.' His primary school prepared those children who planned to go on to grammar school for the 11-plus exam and Ben further explained that out of his class of 35 about 15 to 20 sat the exam, of whom eight to ten passed. Five in total went from his class to the grammar school that Ben attended.

Ben had parents who encouraged him to achieve academically and a teacher who was also proactive in encouraging him and others in his class to make certain secondary school choices. She prepared them for the 11-plus exam, as passing this exam was a prerequisite for obtaining entrance to these academically selective schools.

One participant, Craig, went to his local secondary school for GCSEs and then to a private grammar school for the sixth form. The funds for this were made available by his mother's partner, Jim. Craig explained that:

Jim was interested in academic things … he always tells me he loves John Donne poetry but was not interested in school … and regrets that he didn't spend his intelligence wisely and so in a way channels that into me. And he said: 'Right Craig you might not be my son but I am going to give you all the money I possibly can and we are going to get you good qualifications, we will get you the best possible start in life.'

Jim actively encouraged Craig to apply to the private grammar school, so he did, and he was, after an interview process, offered a place. Jim provided the economic capital to make this possible. These changes in the family capital enabled Craig to attend a school that had a history of sending students deemed to be academically able to elite universities.

When it came to choosing a secondary school for Graham, his mother chose a school outside their catchment area that was oversubscribed. Graham recounted the experience:

I mean it was almost like impossible to get into the secondary school that I wanted to get into. It was either that one or one that was absolutely terrible … it was almost like court cases and things with various parents struggling to get into this school, but I got lucky with that.

Four participants went to secondary schools that had religious affiliations. The consensus among these young men was that their parents considered these schools to be 'better' than the local comprehensives. It appears that the parents of the seven young men referred to above had the cultural capital necessary to understand the importance of ensuring that their children attended schools that they saw as offering their children 'better' educational opportunities.

Some parents left the choice of schools to the child, as was the case with one participant, Karl. He explained that: 'I just chose it [the secondary school] because that was the school I liked the look of.' He was the only child from his primary school to go to that school. For him the choice of secondary school was made almost randomly because he 'kind of decided yes, I like that school, it looks like fun, I think I want to go here'. This is far from some middle-class children's experiences, where parents plan the transition to secondary school sometimes with an almost military precision, even buying houses in the catchment area of a good school (Gewirtz *et al.*, 1995).

Mark's mother put the family home on the market as she wanted to move house to live in the catchment area of what she perceived as a 'better' secondary school. She had stayed on at school until she was 18 and had been a business advisor in a job centre until she was made redundant (this redundancy occurred while Mark was at university), and appeared to have the economic as well as cultural capital of the kind available to many middle-class families. As Vincent (2001) says: 'middle-class parents can call upon resources of social, cultural and economic capital in order to exercise their voice over education issues' (p. 360). As it happened, Mark and his parents did not end up moving as Mark was adamant that he wanted to go to the same secondary school as his friends. He recalled his father saying: 'Well, if he doesn't want to go then he can go to this one' (the local secondary school, Mark's choice). Unusually, his mother was overruled.

Some of the parents did not engage with the choice process. Craig told me that his mother never thought of the possibility of sending him to a secondary school other than the local one. As he recalled: 'I went where everyone else went. A comprehensive that was in special measures when I went there … under 20 per cent of people passed their GCSEs.'

Seven young men went to one or other of the comprehensive schools local to them. Some of these comprehensive schools were known *not* to be so-called 'good' schools and two were in 'special measures'. According to the Office for Standards in Education, Children's Services and Skills (Ofsted), schools require special measures when they are failing to give pupils an acceptable standard of education (2008). Oliver recalled that student behaviour was a problem at his secondary school: 'One teacher had her fingers broken by a student in a door because she wouldn't let us go to lunch.'

So, one could ask why these parents did not choose another school for their children. We know that parents are given some choice over which school their children can attend. In reality, this choice of a 'better' school is not always readily available to all. In the policy and popular rhetoric on parental choice, little attention is focused on the constraints faced by parents with minimum economic resources and diminished social power. Parents do not all make their choices under the same circumstances. For example, those existing on income support, living in certain areas, and reliant on public transport will not have the same range of schools available and accessible to them (David *et al.*, 1996).

In my study, there appear to be some parents who had the cultural knowledge and social connections to understand the importance of choosing a school and who possessed the economic capital to fund the travel to a school outside the catchment area, whereas others perhaps lacked the cultural capital and/or the economic capital that enable choice (Allen *et al.*, 2014).

This was definitely the case for many of these young men. When I asked him what his parents thought about the problems within his secondary school, Oliver recalled: 'They didn't think it was ideal but there is not a great deal you can do really.' Graham recalled that the Education Maintenance Allowance [EMA] '…was very useful, I used that to pay the bus fare for me to actually get to college'. Without the EMA, Graham could not have travelled to the sixth-form college with a better academic reputation than the one within walking distance of his home. Graham went on to study physics at an elite university.

Secondary schools and cultures of masculinity
Some forms of hegemonic masculinity can have a detrimental effect on the academic achievement of boys, with these versions of masculinity often being enacted within a peer group. Peer groups can provide a sense of belonging and support and may also influence the individual's attitudes to schooling, behaviour, and academic outcomes. Any males who do not 'fit into' the group's definition of masculinity become '*othered*' (Archer and Yamashita, 2003; Sherriff, 2007; Willis, 1977). The boys who perform these hegemonic masculinities are often able to gain positions of dominance within the

classroom and several of the participants recall the transition to secondary schooling being quite traumatic as they experienced being 'othered'.

Oliver explained that: 'The first couple of years were awful: I absolutely hated it … I was seen as a bit of a geek.' When I asked Frank to describe his secondary school years he simply replied: 'It was an *experience*.' In their secondary schools, these two young men faced a habitus with which they were not familiar. Oliver recalled that in 'Year 9 I started making a couple more friends, so I probably went down the wrong track a little bit, started smoking, yes thought I was cool'. Oliver discovered that if he became part of the dominant peer group he was no longer bullied. He also recalled that his studies suffered somewhat but his mother insisted that he study when at home. In this way, Oliver did well academically at GCSE level while maintaining status within his peer group. While Frank was in Years 7 and 8, he was very much part of the peer group engaging in dominant anti-school masculinities; in his own words, he 'just mucked about, got into fights and stuff'. However, on reading his Year 8 report he thought: 'Why am I being a dick? I want to go to university and I am just ruining it for myself.'

Most of the young men talked of the pressure to engage in boisterous anti-school behaviour to fit in. Many of them emphasized that they did not socialize with the boys who engaged in these activities. Craig, for instance, spent break times in the school library to avoid contact with 'the lads'. Some participants were somewhat engaged in a sports-masculinity discourse through their participation in football/rugby. They all emphasized the importance of doing well educationally and this was a major focus for them.

In general, white working-class boys underperform in terms of their academic ability and potential for academic attainment; they are considered problematic in educational terms. However, all of the young men who participated obtained the necessary GCSE qualifications to continue their education into the sixth form. Indeed, eight of them achieved predominantly A*and A grades at GCSE level, three of the others achieved predominantly Bs and Cs, while the other four achieved mainly Cs and Ds.

Overall, the young men managed to 'buck the trend' and moved from compulsory education to further education fairly seamlessly. Only Edward had to change his plans for further education when he received his GCSE results. Originally, he had planned to stay on at his Roman Catholic secondary school, but because his 'results were the worst of my life, probably … a massive wake-up call … it was a bad day', he had to re-evaluate his situation. His aunt suggested to him that he apply to a sixth-form college that offered a BTEC in sport. She provided the cultural knowledge about further education that he lacked, and he took this new knowledge and worked with it.

While the institutional habitus of some of the schools my cohort attended was not always conducive to achieving academic success, this changed for most of them on entering the sixth form. As Leon explained:

> Most people are there [in the sixth form] for a good reason ...
> The discipline problem is partly resolved ... they don't think you
> are odd if you are exceptionally good because most people are.

Most of the young people who stayed on at school beyond the compulsory leaving age did so because they wanted to go on to some form of higher education. This was a cohort who generally valued education. Many of the discipline problems that occurred in the early years of secondary school, as described by the participants, appeared to lessen once they were in further education. Those who had described themselves as 'geeks' (as Craig said: 'I was always picked on because I was goofy') earlier on in secondary school found themselves with more like-minded students in the post-compulsory setting of the sixth form or further education college. In some ways, it seemed as if the dominant forms of masculinity that many of the respondents reported in the compulsory school setting were replaced by a pro-school, pro-schoolwork ethic in their sixth forms. It was acceptable and not uncommon to be a 'geek'.

Seven of the participants experienced what would be considered conventional A level routes to university, attending elite universities. Six came through the BTEC programme and studied at modern universities, while one participant, Karl, came through an access programme and attended a modern university. Only one young man interviewed at a modern university had come through the traditional A level route.

Parental involvement in secondary schooling

While some parents did actively help their sons with their academic work, the majority seemed to take a back seat once they went on to secondary school. Parents would encourage their sons to do the set homework and sometimes extra study instead of playing outdoors with their friends. However, the parents did not get involved with the curriculum, teaching methods, or any other aspect of their son's schooling. Not one of the participants could recall their parents being involved in any aspect of their secondary schooling.

Generally, the respondents' mothers, while very supportive of their sons' academic advancement, did not feel they had the academic competences to help them. Like the mothers in Reay's 2005 study, they did not have the cultural capital that enabled them to support their children's academic progress and neither did they feel competent in speaking with their children's teachers as this was a habitus with which they were uncomfortable (Reay *et al.*, 2010). As Graham explained when asked what role his mother played in his secondary schooling: 'She was supportive of whatever I wanted to do and she would just encourage me to go as far as I could go basically.'

Academic alternatives

There are many studies which suggest that football is much more important to many working-class young men than almost anything else, including education (Francis, 1999; Power *et al.*, 1998; Smith, 2007). From the viewpoint of their peers, the boys who were good at football were seen as 'cool' and 'hard'. This reputation gained them the respect of their peers, which was much more important than gaining recognition through academic achievement (Power *et al.*, 1998). Footballing prowess provided the boys with the ultimate 'successful' identity and the boys who excelled at football earned 'physical capital' (Smith, 2007).

Several of the young men's positive memories of their schooling were to do with sport and sometimes sports teachers. David recalled that the teacher who stood out for him at school was his Year 6 teacher, who was also the PE teacher and football coach. Six of them played football and one played rugby. David recounted that: '[I] was really good at football, so I dominated the football team.' Mark played football for his county and he told me: 'I got As in my sports, I was always close to my sports teachers and I was captain of the football team.' Some, like Harvey, found that the football crowd were not the academic type. He recalled that:

> The people I hung around with didn't like, they weren't really the academic sort, mainly football people. That is why I hung around with them to play football etc. And they were, like I say, always saying are you coming out? And I was like, I've got to do this [homework]. As I got older I think I went away with them more.

Harvey went on to say that as he got older he tended to do his homework 'more last minute'. The young men who played football/rugby gained the respect of their peers, but they did engage with academic study often because their mothers would ensure that homework and revision work were completed.

These seven young men did go on to higher education and five of them successfully completed a sports degree. Football/rugby did not replace academic achievement; it became part of their academic profile. This specific group accessed universities that accepted BTEC qualifications in sport and offered courses that encompassed their passion – football/rugby. Most of them were encouraged to go on to university by their teachers in the sixth form, but they were often left to do their own research into what and where they could study given their qualifications. All seven attended a modern university and studied sports science. They were able to convert their sporting capital into a form of academic capital.

University choice

Generally, the young men and their parents believed that education led to social mobility, even if they did not express it this way. While one participant had a parent who had gone to university, most parents left school at the legal leaving age and some even earlier. Consequently, when their sons were applying to university, many of the parents did not have the social capital to access information about higher education that is available to middle-class parents and to parents who have been to university themselves (Smyth and Banks, 2012). Knowledge about university entrance and courses offered is not easily available at home for those who are first-generation university students. Their parents had the cultural capital to know that undergraduate degrees traditionally guaranteed a good job with a good salary. But they perhaps did not fully understand what Grenfell and James (1998) refer to as *qualification inflation*, where over time certification such as a degree no longer guarantees the same jobs or salary as could once be expected.

Many of the parents did not seem to have acquired the capital needed to distinguish between the different types of university and the options they offer. They did not appear to understand that all universities are not equal and that the job opportunities available to graduates from different universities are also different.

The seven young men who had attended elite universities had all been advised by their teachers in the sixth form that they should apply to an elite university. For most of them and their parents the possibility of going to one of these institutions had never occurred to them until then. As Craig explained:

> The teachers are incredibly supportive ... and basically were like, you have got the grades for it, do it. So I did and I got in and I just think it is mad considering that no one else in my family has gone to higher education.

Progressing to higher education ... another tale

The progression into higher education for the young men was never straightforward and some faced more obstacles than others. Some, such as Edward, spent three years in the sixth form in order to obtain the necessary qualifications to attend university. He was originally going to stay on at his school, but, as we saw, did not get the necessary marks at GCSE level to do so and he spent three years at FE college. He informed me that in the first year he did:

> the first diploma and then that was just to get on the real one, the national diploma. I got a distinction, merit, merit ... it is 280 UCAS points so it is quite good. I think the BTEC is an easy way to get into university. Being honest, if I had done A levels, I don't think I would be at a university like this because of the pressure and the exams because the BTEC is 100 per cent coursework.

Edward is at university because he had an aunt who introduced him to the possibility of getting into university through an alternative to the traditional A level route. She had the cultural knowledge and he had the desire to go to university whatever it took. He was not daunted by the prospect of having to do three years at college instead of two. Edward's data showed that there was room for agency.

Adam came from a small village, went to the local primary school, and the closest secondary school to his village. Of the 130 students in his secondary school year group, 30 went into the sixth form and five then went on to university. At GCSE level, Adam attained ten A*s and one A. He recalled that after he did his mock GCSEs and did well it occurred to him that he was academically bright. For A level he chose maths, further maths, physics, and English literature. He dropped English literature after his AS level exams and he explained that doing the further maths: 'was quite hard because our school didn't have a further maths teacher or somebody who was willing to teach further maths ... so I decided to teach myself'. In Year 13 Adam was elected head boy of the school and he discovered that he was the only student to continue with the physics course. The other seven students studying physics dropped it after getting Us in their AS exams. 'So that went down to just an hour of teaching a week,' he said. He was self-taught in further maths and receiving one hour a week of physics tuition.

The head of sixth form encouraged him and three other students to apply to an elite university. This had never occurred to Adam and he recalled that:

> Our head of sixth form sat us down and said, 'I want you all to
> seriously consider these elite universities.' She was really good …
> she was the one who persuaded us and when I came on the open
> day, I really enjoyed it but still never thought that I would get in
> or had a chance of getting in.

Adam attained two A*s and an A at A levels and he went on to study
engineering at an elite university.

Ben went to an all-boys state grammar school and did the International
Baccalaureate there. He chose this qualification rather than the A level
route, even though it was new to the school, because: 'I knew at this point
I would be applying to an elite university. I think I knew I didn't want to
be another three-A candidate.' He received an offer from an elite university
that required him to achieve two 7s at higher level with an overall offer of
40. Ben achieved an overall score of 42 but received only one 7 and two 6s
at higher level, therefore not attaining the target. The head of sixth form at
his school phoned the university on Ben's behalf and Ben was told to ask for
a re-mark of the papers. This he did, but one of his history papers had been
lost by the markers and therefore his mark did not go up. Ben said:

> Obviously I phoned up [the university] and explained the
> situation and said what had happened … so the tutor went and
> spoke to the senior tutors that day and phoned me the following
> day and said, 'Congratulations you've got your place!'

Ben had the determination to press on with his ambition of attending
an elite university. He also had access to his teacher's cultural and social
capital. This teacher was prepared to make the initial telephone call to the
university. Both Ben and his teacher understood the unwritten 'rules of the
game' (Maton, 2008: 57). This was a case of habitus matching social field.

Not all of the young men went straight from school to university.
Two of the participants, Nathan and Oliver, had initially decided not to go
to university. Nathan went straight to work after successfully completing a
BTEC in sport, but after a year spent working in a supermarket he applied
to university. Oliver also went straight to work from school:

> Because Dad sort of knows what he is talking about with money
> so, I was just like follow that kind of thing and not go to university
> and as it is such a lot of money, a waste of money kind of thing.

However, Oliver visited a friend at university and after that visit he decided
to apply too. He told me: 'I saw what university was like, I was like I've got

to go to university, I have got to go, I don't care where I go or what I do, I have got to go.' Oliver was also the only participant attending a modern university who had taken A levels (six of the other participants at modern universities completed a BTEC and one entered university through an access programme). In his second year of university, Oliver had severe personal and emotional problems and left university to return the following year. On his return, he discovered that the programme he had originally been on, a Qualified Teacher Status (QTS) programme, was no longer on offer and he was offered a place on the sports science programme instead.

Another participant, Edward, had originally enrolled at a modern university only to withdraw after the first term. He then accepted a place the next academic year at a different modern university, which is where I met him. The reason he gave for leaving the original university was that he wanted to live at home.

Conclusion

The young men in my study all came from families who valued education but most of their siblings did not go on to university and this speaks of their agency. They all experienced academic success early and this seemed to have stood them in good stead when many of them found themselves in challenging secondary schools and situations. Mentor teachers played an important if not fundamental role in the academic lives of the participants – progression to university would in many cases not have happened without these mentors, who played an instrumental role in the academic trajectories of the young men. The seven participants who obtained entrance to an elite university would never have applied without the encouragement of their teachers.

All 15 stories tell of achievement *against the odds*. All needed persistence, resilience, and sheer determination at various stages in their schooling. All 15 had to manoeuvre their way through a system that was littered with obstacles. Arrival at the destination – university – was never a given but was a hard-earned achievement. It is little wonder then that in the academic year 2011/12 (the year that the young men entered university), only 21 per cent of all young people who had been on free school meals entered university (DfE, 2016b).

Chapter 4

Experiences at university

> *These ... working-class students have developed almost superhuman levels of motivation, resilience and determination ... They have managed to achieve considerable success as learners and acquire the self-confidence and self-regulation that accompanies academic success against the odds.*
>
> (Reay *et al.*, 2009: 1115)

Having explored how the young men successfully negotiated their way through the school system, this chapter focuses on their experiences during the first two years of university. What became immediately apparent during the second round of interviews was that they all experienced apprehension on entering the unfamiliar university environment; they were 'like fish out of water' (Bourdieu, 1984).

Although many experiences were common to all participants, many were also substantially different, depending on the type of university attended. The key themes are clustered into three codes: similarities, differences, and discrepant cases.

Seven of the participants went to one or other of two elite universities and studied a range of subjects, seven went to the same modern university where they studied sports science, and one participant attended another modern university and studied education (see Table 4.1).

Table 4.1: Name of participants and type of university attended

Name	Type of university
Adam	Elite
Ben	Elite
Craig	Elite
Graham	Elite
Ian	Elite
John	Elite
Leon	Elite
David	Modern

Name	Type of university
Edward	Modern
Frank	Modern
Harvey	Modern
Karl	Modern
Mark	Modern
Nathan	Modern
Oliver	Modern

Commonalities

Difficulties with the 'rules of the game' and the 'institutional habitus'

All of the young men experienced a degree of apprehension when they first started university. They all reported experiencing difficulties in negotiating the rules of the game of university life (Bourdieu, 1990b). While the culture within the universities is different and each institution has its own set of practices and discourses that comprise its institutional habitus, these had to be negotiated by the young men. They found they did not have available to them the cultural capital necessary to adapt to this new habitus seamlessly.

Once at university, they found they had to learn the 'new rules of the game'. Adam (elite) recalled that in his first year he:

> ... had been just thrown in a bit and [did] not really know what to expect ... at the beginning it was quite hard just because there are a lot of people who came from private schools and towards the beginning I wasn't sure I should be coming here ... I remember my brother calling me ... the people I was sat by ... were comparing ski resorts ... I was like I should not be here.

Mark (modern) said:

> The first year was very hard for me because I am quite close to my mum and dad ... I still have thoughts of if I'd stayed home and done something else. But I'm glad I did it in the end, it is just ... it is more ... the detail you have to put into your work, the amount of literature that you need to go and read.

These examples illustrate that Adam and Mark had limited experience of the culture of higher education, its structure, and organization – its 'institutional habitus'. They had very limited knowledge of what to expect or what to do once they arrived at university and they found that their habitus and the field or social space of the university were mismatched. This is what Bourdieu (1990b) refers to as 'situations of crisis which disrupt the immediate adjustment of habitus to field' (p. 109). All of the participants initially felt as Adam and Mark did, thinking 'this is not for me'. However, except for John (elite), they transformed their habitus and adjusted to the situation.

By the end of the second year, most of the young men had settled into their university lives and most had adapted to the academic culture and the institutional habitus of their university. They were more like fish in water, their habitus matching the field. They had become attuned to the *doxa*, the unwritten rules of the university. As Craig (elite) recounted:

> Oh, it has been a lot better than last year ... obviously you get more settled in your second year. You know what you are up to, what is expected of you, so yes it has been good and ... I am not so stabbing in the dark ... I would describe it as settled, as successful, as fun.

When Frank (modern) was asked to describe his second year at university, he replied: 'It has been fun, it has been eventful, it has been really eventful but it has been fun.' It should be added that while most of the young men had adapted to university life, they did so with varying degrees of success, and this aspect is explored later in the chapter.

All but three of the participants were living away from home. The seven attending the elite universities were living either in halls or in houses owned by their respective colleges. Of the eight attending the modern universities, three lived at home, though one of these, Harvey, lived in halls in his first year but then chose to live at home for economic reasons in the second year. Another two also lived at home for economic as well as 'attachment' reasons. Frank was a Senior Resident in halls and the other four lived in houses near the university.

Most of the young men talked about initially being homesick. As Craig recalled: 'You live away from home ... so you have no experience of how this works and it is a worry ... it is a big change ... I was missing home and things like that.' Frank told me: 'I got really homesick to start with.' Perhaps this also happens to middle-class students, but generally they have been prepared for the intricacies of going away to university and while they may be homesick, they understand the process, whereas working-class students have 'no experience of how this works' (Craig).

Most of the young men felt that socially they had adapted well by the end of the second year and most attending the modern universities said they had had no difficulties adapting socially from the beginning. As Mark recounted: 'I got quite close to the people I was in halls with ... so it is quite good socially here.'

Most of the young men expressed initial doubts about their suitability to attend university, often because of their reservations about their working-class backgrounds. As both Leon and Adam recalled:

> Socially I thought I was going to be very intimidated by it, but I made friends very quickly ... I found it much better than I thought I would ... whilst you imagine it is going to be a public school hotspot it is actually a more diverse range of people than you will get anywhere else and that is such a brilliant thing.
>
> (Leon, elite)

> I thought it was going to be really snobby when I first arrived but it is quite normal, if not a typical university experience, but then again that is not why people come here.
>
> (Adam, elite)

All of the students reported that in their first year they found university challenging and in many cases suffered a crisis of confidence. Those at the elite universities were particularly intimidated because they had all been the 'best' in their classes at school and at university they found themselves surrounded by equally clever people. As John recalled:

> When doing my A levels and GCSEs I just kind of went to classes and turned up at the exams and that was about it ... here I kind of struggled with [not being the best] ... I think I have done okay ... I think I am quite middle really ... It is new, I am not used to it. I am kind of used to being at the top but you know I have learned to cope with it.

Craig also recalled: 'All of a sudden I am not the best ... suddenly in tutorials I can't answer all of the questions and people answer it before me ... I don't enjoy it.'

Ian remarked that: 'Coming here has given me some humility as well, which is really good.' But this was not unique to those attending the elite universities; those attending modern universities also reported finding the work difficult. Frank recalled that the mark he received for his first essay was very disappointing, so he went and had a chat with his tutor:

> ... and he basically said this is what you need to do when you
> write an essay and I realized after that mark, yes, no, university is
> all about self-learning ... you have to go away and research.

Nathan told me: 'At first I found it quite difficult but as soon as you get the hang of how the writing style is different and referencing and everything then it is not so bad.' These working-class young men, apart from Ben (elite), came to university as the first in their families to do so and had not been exposed to the 'linguistic capital' needed to succeed in higher education institutions. They had difficulties with the academic language as well as the style of teaching (Bourdieu and Passeron, 1977).

Adam (elite) explained that the teaching at his school (a comprehensive school in a former mining town) was very different from the teaching at his elite university, but that his university friends who had attended public schools told him that: 'They were taught what to do and how ... they had tutorials and supervisions [at school].' They had been armed with the necessary linguistic, social, and cultural capital to make a relatively effortless transition to university. This is not to say that all middle-class students necessarily make the transition seamlessly.

One reason educational inequalities occur is because first-generation working-class students do not have the linguistic code, the particular language of the higher educational institution. This must be acquired by the new students. Once this code is learned, it can be transformed into 'scholastic capital' (Bourdieu and Passeron, 1977).

Broadening of horizons and the appearance of social differences between participants and their 'home' contacts

Most of the young men I interviewed spoke about university broadening their horizons and changing their perceptions. Ian (elite) explained that:

> People here have elevated the level of debate for some reason ...
> the complexity of conversation is a lot higher ... I don't want to
> feel that I am above them when I go back [home] ... I really have
> to change between home and uni.

Ian found that the language of his home habitus was different from the language of the university habitus. He engaged in 'code switching'. This occurs when a speaker alternates between two or more languages, language varieties, or dialects and styles (DeBose, 1992). Some of the young men found themselves using different 'styles' of language in different environments. The language they used at home was different from the language they used at university. Ian found that he engaged with one language code at home and another at university, and the same was the case for David (modern):

> I'm here and you are meeting new people and ... [the] social experience you get, you learn what is appropriate to say where some of them at home, like they have just been isolated for so long, they just don't communicate appropriately, you know what I mean? It just seems like awkward, I mean I get along with them but if they are in a bigger crowd ... they just are socially not right ... I have just become more independent, I don't know really, I am just becoming my own person and they are still like ... They are just still finding themselves.

Most of the young men found themselves moving in two different social worlds, as Adam (elite) observed: 'University and home just move at a totally different pace', and Nathan (modern) said: 'When you are at home it is like nothing has changed!' Edward (modern) said that his friends:

> go on the same holidays ... do the same things at weekends. ... It is just ridiculous, whereas I want to experience everything in the world like ... I have started to watch more documentaries ... whether it is David Attenborough ... other shows like that and you just see the world and think why would I want to be stuck ... why would I want to be here all the time?

These students appear to be refashioning themselves in the wake of their experiences at university (Bourdieu, 1990b). So while their habitus is being modified by their experiences at university, they are still retaining their links with their home habitus (Reay *et al.*, 2009). All of the participants reported that they had developed different perspectives and priorities and now had an engagement with an intellectual world that their university experiences had opened for them.

Very few of the young men mixed with their university friends outside university. As Harvey (modern) informed me: 'At uni I have got my uni friends and when I go back home, I have got my normal friends.' This comment by Harvey that his home friends are his 'normal' friends was intriguing. He still saw his home life, which equates to his working-class life, as somewhat more 'normal' than the habitus of university. Perhaps Harvey still felt like a cultural outsider at university. Mark (modern) told me that most of the people he mixed with at university 'have all got a big friendship group at home as in, back where they live'. These young men have two lives, which they have learned to compartmentalize, keeping them separate but coexisting in harmony (Aries and Seider, 2005).

Only two, Ben (elite) and Ian (elite), said that they mixed with university friends in their holidays: 'There is probably a group of about six of us and we go and stay at each other's houses' (Ben). Perhaps these young men have successfully integrated socially into their new habitus or are more confident about their working-class backgrounds. These two young men appeared not to feel inferior in relation to their working-class habitus. They had adopted the habitus of the new but were at ease with where they had come from; for them, the transition appeared to have been smooth and they seemed to be able to move between the two different fields with ease (Lehmann, 2012). As Leon (elite) remarked: 'I don't feel as alienated as it would suggest with two different lives, but, yes, they are different spheres.'

The value of education and achieving a 2:1

All of the young men valued education. Several said that they valued higher education because it provided them with the ability to become mobile. When Frank (modern) was asked why he valued education, his response was:

> I just wanted to get out of Riverton [pseudonym for the name of the town he grew up in], I didn't want to spend my life there. Don't get me wrong, it is nice. You see people around town and you see the people stuck in dead-end jobs that they hate ... like I just don't want to be stuck in the same town for the rest of my life.

Leon (elite) expressed similar feelings:

> I think, like always feeling a bit sort of outside of people who lived locally who were like, had done the same job for like 50 years and read the *Daily Mail* and this, and, never really like understanding that mindset much and always wanting something different to that to some degree. I am not saying I'm trying to rise above something.

All of the participants who referred to having changed or who had said that they wished to move on were also very quick to point out that they did not think there was anything wrong with where they had come from, as can be seen from both Frank and Leon's quotes. They did not want to appear as if they thought that they were superior to those at home or were being judgemental.

The young men all understood the importance of achieving at least a 2:1 in their degree to secure future employment. They had learned that being at university was about more than achieving a pass. Craig (elite) said that he was hoping to work in the civil service: 'They put you through a few kind of hoops in your final year to see if they definitely want to take you on, so you have to get a 2:1.'

All of the participants understood that, in the current economic climate in the UK, employment opportunities were difficult to obtain. The young men who were considering postgraduate study also understood that they needed at least a 2:1 or in some cases a first. They had come to understand the dispositions of this field, the rules of the game. They understood that the degree they were studying for had an exchange value in the workplace depending on the mark obtained and that it had a different value from other degrees. Those at the modern universities understood that their degrees were subject-specific and that the career options open to them would be in the field of study they were undertaking. Therefore, the young men studying sports science saw themselves going into some sport-related occupation such as football coaching or PE teaching, and the young man studying education saw himself following a career in that field.

Not all of them were planning to leave university on completion of their degree. Graham (elite) was on course to achieve a first and he planned to do a PhD. Leon (elite) had planned to do a master's programme at his university and he understood that: 'Unless you get a first, you basically don't get offered a place.' Some of the young men at one of the modern universities had hoped to get on to the PGCE course at their university. To do this they required a first.

These then are some of the commonalities experienced by these first-generation white working-class male university students. There are also differences in their experiences and none more so than that of the degree of belonging experienced at the different types of university. Each type of university has its own institutional habitus, which influences the students' learner and class identities to a greater or lesser extent (Reay *et al.*, 2010).

Differences
Levels of immersion in life at university and attachment to locality
Those young men who had attended elite universities were immersed in university life during term time and said that they spent extra time at the university in their holidays, usually to prepare readings, assignments, or dissertations before term began. As Craig remarked:

> I'm coming back to university [early] mainly because I'll have to start reading ... recap the stuff I've done this year and I'll have

exams when I come back, not real ones but ones I'll still need to revise for.

Adam told me that: 'I think I've *immersed* myself quite well into college life and there are lots of societies that you can be part of if you manage your time well.'

These young men were provided with university accommodation for the three years they were at university. They had more contact hours per week than their peers at the modern universities. Adam recalled that one week he had 42 contact hours, whereas Nathan (modern) told me: 'I've only had two modules [this semester] so four contact hours a week, which is a struggle to keep yourself entertained sometimes.' David (modern) said that he had 11 contact hours per week and this appeared to be the norm at the modern universities the young men attended.

At the elite universities, students had a tutorial session for each of their modules every week. These sessions normally involved two or three students meeting up with a lecturer to discuss the essays they had completed that week. At the modern universities, tutorials were held very infrequently and with much larger groups. Karl (modern) said that he only had 'tutorials after the essays where they go through the papers with us'. The workload was much heavier at the elite universities, with most students having to write at least two essays a week, whereas the norm at modern universities was four or five a semester.

Modern universities offered approximately 11 hours of non-compulsory lectures each week and tutorials infrequently, therefore giving students little contact time with the academic staff. This means the first-generation students who come to university with little educational capital take longer than their counterparts at the elite universities to learn the rules of academia (Crozier and Reay, 2011: 149).

Many of the young men at modern universities had failed essays, received little feedback, and then resat any failed essays at the end of the academic year. The system at modern universities is less structured than that of the elite universities and while the young men at the modern university could ask for help, they rarely did. Most of them felt it was up to themselves to sort out their difficulties, as Harvey observed: 'But I should learn from my mistake.' Students were required to be proactive in seeking support and most of them had difficulty doing this. This belief among the young men at the modern universities that they had to sort out their own problems resulted in many of them not doing as well academically as they might have. It is possible to speculate that when dominant masculine discourses encourage men to see seeking help as 'feminine', such reticence is counterproductive in the university setting.

Another difference related to how the young men socialized during term time. Many of those attending modern universities said that they did not spend much time socializing at university as they still maintained ties with their family and friends from home. David said that: 'I go home quite a lot on Saturday night just to go and play football.' Mark told me: 'I've been getting *stressed*, so I go home to do a bit of work at Mum and Dad's.' This attachment to *locality* is evident in many studies with working-class communities. For working-class young men, this sense of belonging within a locality brings with it a sense of security and belonging, as well as a strong social network (Ingram, 2009). This was apparent in most of those young men at the modern universities maintaining close ties to family and locality. As Edward (modern) said:

> I wanted to stay at home, to be honest ... I didn't see a point of me living here when I could stay at home and also, yes I think that was it, I just wanted to live at home to be honest.

Many of the young men who had attended the modern universities chose a university that was not too far away from home. When I asked Mark (modern) why he had chosen the university he is now attending, he recalled that: 'It was quite a big decision if you are going to be moving away. I didn't want to be too far, like [names a university in the north of the country].' David (modern) told me that he applied to: 'The closest one [university] because obviously I wanted to come home to play football and that.'

Most of those attending modern universities were strongly attached to family and friends, who provided emotional security during the initial period of turmoil they faced in their first year of university. They actively appeared to choose their families as their major source of emotional support, but it could also be plausible that this attachment may have been more about the bonds these young men had with their local male friends and football club than family.

Work, holiday reading, work experience, and future career plans

Most of the young men who attended elite universities studied through their holidays; this usually involved reading in preparation for the following term's lectures. Those who attended modern universities rarely did any study in their holidays, though they understood that they would benefit from doing extra reading and research.

Some of the young men attending modern universities worked part time in term time, as well as through the holidays. Those at the elite universities were not permitted to work in term time and were provided with bursaries so that they did not have to work in the Christmas or Easter breaks, as Ian remarked:

> There is a vacation grant which is £500 for the Christmas vacation and £500 for the Easter vacation that is provided by the college. That is so we don't feel like we have to get jobs when we go home because my parents were kind of pushing me towards getting a job and that scholarship kind of said like, let me do my work over the holidays because it takes me the whole holiday to do my revision and reading and get things sorted.

In the summer holiday between the participants' second and third year of study, all but one young man did some form of work. Those at the modern universities did not normally undertake work that was related to their degree. They tended to work in bars, as labourers, at theme parks, and the like. Nathan told me that his summer holiday work was 'a job as a steward or a job as a waiter'. Edward commented: 'I don't know, it might be at the new place, the bookmakers.' This paid work was an economic necessity for these students. I asked the young men about doing work in their holidays that may enhance their chances of obtaining future employment in their chosen field. Their stock answer to my question was 'no', even though on further probing some of them did say that they could perhaps do some work that would enhance their CVs, but it was not a major consideration. They were concerned primarily with earning money.

Only Frank did work that was a helpful addition to his CV. He was also the only student attending a modern university who had been to see the careers advisor on campus. He said that he had been told by the careers advisor to build up work experience that was relevant to the teaching of PE, this being the career he aspired to. In visiting the careers advisory centre, Frank had tapped into the social and cultural capital of the careers advisor. While Frank was the exception among those from the modern universities, those at the elite universities almost always found internships that would be a useful addition to their CVs, as Craig remarked:

> I will be working in the Department of Transport, which is where I've been assigned for six to nine weeks, and it is paid because it is a university internship. So it is aimed at students who can't support themselves and it is in London.

I asked the young men attending elite universities how they had acquired this knowledge about the need to build up their CVs with internships and work experience. Two extracts are included here as a flavour of the general response I received from them all.

Craig said: 'I suppose a lot of people start talking about it around college and you think oh I better do something about it.'

And Ben said:

> You sort of hear about it because in about the first term all the law firms run loads of events up here ... and because Michaelmas term is recruitment season and there is a big law fair organized by the careers service for the faculty.

These young men were in an environment where they learned that there is strong competition for the limited number of professional careers currently available in the UK. They had been immersed in a habitus and field that understood the importance of building a CV, doing internships at the appropriate places, and the need to obtain a first-class degree or an upper second to be considered for a professional career. And while they did not have the economic capital that many of their middle-class peers enjoyed, their colleges ensured that they were paid when on placements. The participants attending elite universities had access to economic, cultural, and social capital, which most working-class students did not.

Another difference between the two groups was evident in what they said about their time-management skills and approach to study. The respondents at the elite universities appeared to be self-disciplined and self-regulated. Adam told me that in his second year:

> I think I've managed my time better in terms of academic and extra stuff ... most people decided to knuckle down a bit this year ... this is the grade they are coming out with when they apply for jobs ... like you've got to push yourself and I think you've got to know how to manage your time and that kind of thing.

Ian had to impose limits on the amount of time he spent studying:

> So I knew I had to organize my time ... so I stopped working at 8 p.m. every day and I haven't worked on Sundays ... Yes that is within, at those times I can't, I don't allow myself to do any work. So I go and socialize with people.

Most of the respondents at the modern universities told me that they needed to plan better. The concept of being an independent learner was a shock to these young men. They had mostly qualified to enter university through the BTEC route, which they understood to be an easier option than the more traditional A level route. As David recalled: 'It was kind of easy, you got like quite a lot of help.' Frank also recalled being helped a lot: 'If I needed help I'd text him [the teacher] and he'd give me the answers.' These young men were unfamiliar with being left to do their own research. The academic culture of their university, the lack of support and guidance, was something they struggled with. While Frank knew that 'University is all about self-learning, all they do is give you the information, you have to go away and research', he did not always plan well enough to do this in an organized manner. Essays were all due at the end of the semester; this often resulted in some essays being done reasonably well and others being rushed to completion, sometimes in a matter of hours, as Frank told me:

> I'd like just, I'd rushed it, I didn't even realize I had the deadline and I found out six hours before, so I had to do 4,000 words in six hours. I managed to get it done but it got 39.

Edward, who claimed he attended virtually no lectures in his first year, told me:

> That is what has held me back a bit you know ... I've got to find a balance [between his paid employment/playing football for outside teams/university studies] next year ... well uni is the main thing next year definitely ... I've really got to start planning ... I talk such a good game, as in I can say I'll plan but I never actually do it ... it is a bit weird, I don't understand.

David described his difficulty: 'You don't do much and then it all kind of comes at once ... it gets on top of you ... things just mount up and then you get a bit down in the dumps ... I just plod on.' These young men did not seek out support and as their BTEC had not provided them with the sort of transferable skills needed for academic essay writing, this proved problematic for most of them.

Two of the students at modern universities reported that they had not been committed to going on to higher education. Harvey told me: 'Like it was mainly her [his mother's] idea to come to uni.' When I asked another student, David, why he decided to go to university he recalled:

> I remember being quite reluctant at first ... but I think, I didn't know what else to do. I didn't have anything else to do and I didn't just want to just sit at home, so I just went I think.

Unlike their peers at the elite universities, the young men attending modern universities did not appear to have well-laid-out career plans. David and Edward were not sure that they would use their degrees when they had completed their studies. They both planned to travel.

Others who had originally intended to do a PGCE course after their undergraduate degree had second thoughts about their careers as they came to the realization that there were limited numbers of places on the PGCE programme and that they may not achieve the results necessary to gain access. Frank, Harvey, Karl, Mark, and Nathan had, in their first interviews, all stated that they wanted to be teachers.

In the second interview, Nathan expressed an interest in being a football coach instead of a teacher and while he did not explain why his career plans had changed, he did acknowledge that his marks were not high enough to obtain entrance onto the PGCE course. This was also the case for Harvey. Karl had decided that he would like to go into the production of education materials and Mark, who still had ambitions to be a teacher, stated: 'By the time I've finished, there might be something available to me that is different and suits me more, but a PGCE, I don't think would.' His concern was that he would not be able to cope with the level of work; he also understood he needed to achieve a first and this was not a realistic expectation at that stage. Frank was also still set on becoming a teacher and was hoping to be able to do some 'on-the-job training', equivalent to the graduate teacher programme (GTP). Most of the young men who had experienced low academic performance and/or failed an essay or a unit of work changed their career aspirations; however, Frank and Mark maintained their original plans.

Extracurricular activities

All of the young men had participated in extracurricular activities, but there were differences in the nature and location of these. Those at the elite universities were fully embedded in university life during term time; the extracurricular activities they engaged in took place at university and were not generally sporting in nature – they were often related to the subjects they were studying.

The only young man at a modern university not participating in extracurricular sporting activities was Karl, who was also the only one at a modern university reading education. He told me that a lot of his spare time was taken up being 'a Scout leader and a Beaver Cubs leader'.

The other young men at modern universities were involved in extracurricular sporting activities: for six this was football and for one it was rugby. Those engaged in extracurricular sporting activities were studying sports science at university. They had a passion for sport and appeared to have converted their sporting capital into a form of academic capital, continuing to use their sporting prowess in their spare time and engaging in full-time academic study. These young men appeared to maintain a 'foot in both camps', engaged in a sporting-masculinity discourse through their participation in football/rugby while also continuing with their academic studies.

Another difference became apparent between the two groups of men when they were asked why they participated in the activities that they did. All of the young men at the modern universities gave only one reason: that they enjoyed the activity. At the elite universities, some activities were undertaken because they were enjoyed, while others were undertaken not only because they were enjoyed but also because they could be used to build up CVs. Ben said that in the third term of his second year he had become the President of the Bar Society:

> Which is a society for people with a desire to give information and run events for people who want to go to the bar ... a lot of my time this term isn't spent studying, it is doing that ... it is an extracurricular society but it is legally relevant.

Graham, who studied physics, told me that he was the Secretary of the Space and Astronomy Society and its Outreach Officer. At the Society meetings: 'I get to meet the head of the astrophysics department quite frequently so I am getting PhD points!'

Craig, who had been the Junior Common Room (JCR) President in his second year, explained that being JCR President involved:

> Lots of meetings, lots of emails, but it has also helped me to get other things. This summer I've got an internship coming up in the civil service ... you have to do a telephone interview and the JCR things always come up, they were always asking about it, what did you learn from it, what did you take from it, all that kind of stuff.

According to Crozier and Reay (2011), on arrival at elite universities, first-generation working-class students find that there is clear direction that provides security and clarity. These factors enable the students to develop strong learner identities and behaviours that ensure success. The modern universities offer first-generation working-class students a structure that is loose and intended to be non-threatening and relaxed. In actuality, this loose structure can compound the students' confusion, because of the lack of direction and clarity. For the young men who had attended modern universities, the process of acquiring the necessary cultural capital to succeed at university took considerable time; in fact, the process took longer for them than their counterparts at the elite universities.

The somewhat discrepant cases

In my analysis of the second set of interviews, it became apparent that three students' experiences were significantly different from their peers at the same type of university. Thus I described them as discrepant cases: Frank was at a modern university and immersed in life at university; he has had a pronounced 'identity transformation'. John was at an elite university and was the only one in my cohort at elite universities who had not adapted very well to university life. David was at a modern university and was the only student across the spectrum unconvinced that being at university was a worthwhile activity.

Frank displayed characteristics that were like those displayed by students attending elite universities. He had remained in halls while undertaking his degree and in his second and third years he took on the role of Senior Resident in his halls. He also stayed in halls in the summer holiday between his second and third year of study and he worked at a locally based club that taught sports to young children. The extracurricular activities he participated in – rugby, badminton, and drama – were all university-based clubs. The question is, why did Frank so fully embrace life away from home when most of his fellow white working-class males remained more attached to home? Frank was brought up by his mother and has had little contact with his father, who is a taxi driver. He has an older sister who works at a fast-food outlet and a brother who works in a hotel, both of them some ten years older than he is. His mother is a manager at a supermarket local to home. He said: 'I mean my Mum earns, what £12,000 a year before tax and my brother earns £13,000.' Home is a town in Riverton and his brother and sister still live at home. He went on to say that:

> Mum has mollycoddled us, which is why I don't think my brother and sister have left home … I don't know but like I have been the first to say I don't want to be stuck here, I don't want to be living here when I am 30 years old. I want to go and do something, I want to go and be a teacher.

Frank recalled that both his siblings 'bunked off school … but to me education has always been important, always been important'. Frank is a self-motivated young man. He recalled that his mother would have preferred it if he had gone to a university closer to home, but he chose the university he studied at 'because it is far enough away but I can still come back'. His mother called him every day in Freshers' Week to ask him if he was having any problems. It appeared as if Frank's mother was having separation problems. Frank also said that most of the young people he was at school with:

> [W]eren't ready [to move away from home], they like their home comforts ... don't get me wrong I love living at home but I am just so glad I came to university ... so far, yes, it has been the best two years of my life.

Frank did not want to appear to be negative about home, but he felt the need to break with tradition and leave his home town. He has certainly exhibited many of those characteristics that were displayed by the successful working-class young people attending an elite university in the study by Reay *et al.* (2009). These were: 'Almost superhuman levels of motivation, resilience and determination' (p. 1115). When I asked Frank if anyone had encouraged him to do well academically, he told me that he had wanted to be a teacher since:

> I was five, six years old when I ... thought I want to do what they do. I want to help. I love it, I have always loved teaching, I have always loved that feeling you get when you know that someone understands something because of you.

He said that his mother 'is very supportive of that and like yes she has always been there when I've needed her'. Later in the interview, he explained: 'Yes, mum was very, very big on reading ... she would always make time for me to read.' He mentioned his older brother being a replacement father figure for him and he also referred to a teacher in primary school: 'She was a big influence, like whenever I had any problems I would go and see her ... I'm still in contact with [her].' As explained in the previous chapter, Frank went through a period in the first two years of secondary school when he was anything but the ideal student, and a male teacher suggested that if he wanted to get ahead he would have to change his behaviour. Through these two contacts, Frank accumulated the cultural capital necessary to set him apart from most of his peers in his home town.

Frank is extremely determined and single-minded. Failing some essays had not caused him to veer from his initial career aspirations. He did not want to do the PGCE because of the cost, but he remained optimistic that he would obtain a teaching position and then do his teaching qualification while in post. Frank had fully embraced university life.

John, unlike the other participants at elite universities, had problems adjusting to university life. He told me that he had never had to work while at school and would turn up at school on the day of exams: 'And get an A without revising or anything. So I guess I was just lucky in that I could just turn up and not feel pressure in exams and do well.' He went on to say that:

> I thought the hard bit of coming here would be that I was going to be one of the smart people here sort of thing but it is more a case of it doesn't really matter how smart you are, you have to work incredibly hard.

John, like the others, did not know what to expect on arrival at university as a first-generation university student, but unlike the others he never adapted to the new field. He said that in his first year he struggled: '[I] slated myself quite a lot last year, just focusing on work, I really struggled with the social side of things down here.' His second year had not been much better: 'My social life … is non-existent … I haven't really gotten on with anybody since I've come.' Perhaps because he had not socialized while at university, he continued to flounder. He had not become socially comfortable and never acclimatized to the institutional habitus of the university.

John had not come to terms with the fact that he was not the 'best', nor had he learned to cope with the workload or the methods of teaching at his university. As he remarked:

> The work's really quite intense a lot of the time. I don't prepare myself very well … the way they teach is kind of de-motivating compared to what we are used to, in the sense we don't seem to get taught until after we do our work, which always gets to me, that way round.

When I asked him to describe his second year, his response was: 'A lot of hard work really. Sort of prepare, get all the work done, and go home and sleep.' He had no plans for the summer: 'I started to look for some work but I think I left it too late. I'll probably just try and consolidate work and work on getting back to happy again, that sort of thing.' John did not show the self-regulation and self-discipline the other young men at the elite universities displayed. He appeared to spend most of his time studying; he had not found a balance, and said that he was trying to get a first-class degree. His learner identity had not recovered from 'not being the best' and it remained fragile.

John claimed to have adjusted to university life: 'I am used to kind of working all the time now.' But he then went on to say:

> I have a bit of a fear of not like reaching my potential, it feels like an horrific waste if I don't do at least as close to as well as I could do ... If I end up flunking out of university and not making it, my prospects suddenly shoot down massively ... I never seem to live up to my potential and in terms of my general life, I'm pretty ... I'm not in a great place at the moment ... I am just hoping that being here is going to give me a leg up in the future.

John did not adapt to the institutional habitus of the university.

David, who attended a modern university, was the only participant to question the value of a university degree. He said that if he had his time again he would not go to university. He recalled that he just drifted into coming to university because he had nothing else to do:

> If I had known then what I know now, I wouldn't have come ... I know what I could achieve without going [to university] but at the time I didn't, I wasn't really fully developed in the head, I don't think I'd really figured out everything, what I knew about myself.

David told me that 'you don't learn anything of value at university'. He had obviously had this conversation with his father because he then went on to say:

> What my dad says is, you question things because on your course you are constantly questioning. So he says you question things and that is what it [university] teaches you to do, that sort of stuff. But I don't know if I would have ... I don't know if I'd be the same person now but ...

David's older brother, who had left school before he had taken his GCSEs, appeared to have influenced David's thoughts:

> He [his older brother] didn't want to become a wage slave and stuff like that and just, he just, he's done some pretty cool things ... People would look down on him in society because, he just ... drifts about from here to there but really he is seeing new things, experiencing different cultures and things like that. It is really a good life and a bad life.

David faced a conundrum because he knew he had changed, but his question was: has this change occurred because he was attending university or would he have changed anyway? David was experiencing dislocation and, perhaps because of a loyalty to his brother, he was having difficulty justifying the new aspects of himself that had developed while at university.

Discussion

In this section, I first revisit the notion of habitus in relation to the individuals and then in relation to the culture of their higher education institutions (HEIs). It was obvious to me from the outset of the second interview that my cohort was far more assured and confident than they had been in the first meeting. From what they said, it seemed that for the most part they had settled into their university lives and were more like 'fish in water' and had adapted to their university's culture. It was evident from what they said, and how they said it, that this shift included changes in their linguistic codes and their cultural, social, and academic capital. The young men were, in the main, enthusiastic about their university experiences and seemed to be able to move seamlessly between the habitus of their family and their university, although they sometimes made accommodations when returning home.

What emerged strongly was that the cohort reported some significant differences in the habitus of the universities that they attended. Not surprisingly, the elite providers had more resources at their disposal and were able to offer a great deal of support to their working-class undergraduates. Also not surprisingly, given their heritage, tradition, and reputation, they were well networked into postgraduate professional occupational destinations (Power *et al.*, 2003).

Not only were there differences between the institutional habituses of different types of university (elite and modern), but there were also differences in the institutional habituses between similar universities (the two modern providers in my sample). The two modern universities differed in terms of the teaching and support for learning that were on offer. They also differed in terms of the ways in which they seemed to offer an inclusive, caring environment – with one of the universities being in some ways similar, in that respect, to the elite colleges. The other was more detached, with an almost part-time approach towards its student cohort. The point here is that the institutional habitus is a complex phenomenon and cannot easily be reduced to a simple binary such as might be suggested by a contrast between elite and modern HEIs.

The second concept I wish to return to is that of dominant cultures of masculinity and the influences that aspects of these may or may not have played in the academic progress of the young men. As I have discussed in this chapter, some of my sample, particularly those who attended the elite HEIs – but not only, for example, Karl – did not report any dissonances in this arena. For instance, while some of those who attended elite universities had been somewhat marginalized in their earlier school settings (Key Stages 3 and 4) for being 'geeks' and not being sporty, at university they were able to make friends, become influential, and take up mainstream positions (although John was an outlier here).

As I have also argued in this chapter, those young men who attended modern universities and were studying sports sciences had been able to draw on their earlier cultures of masculinity to perform their emergent identities of young graduates. In terms of my wider discussion, here I would like to stress the ways in which dominant versions of masculinity may not be as fixed and immutable as might sometimes be imagined. Masculinity can take different forms, and the versions of masculinity that are on offer as resources for identity construction in HEIs may be more complex and more emotionally versatile and may offer a challenge to some of the more limited versions that exist. Indeed, Gee (2014) talks of what she refers to as 'flexible masculinities' and her case is that role models such as David Beckham 'bend the codes' of masculinity – even in relation to sports. Many of the participants exhibited flexible masculinities: they showed versatility and the ability to construct more nuanced versions of masculinity than those that currently exist.

This point is discussed further in Chapter 6, with the following chapter exploring the young men's final year at university and their career ambitions.

Chapter 5

A degree ... what now?

So if I don't get accepted for the astronaut programme then ... I plan to go on and do a PhD in research.

(Graham)

Job wise I think it'll probably just be something to get by ... a teaching assistant ... like I haven't really started something.

(David)

Initial impressions

My initial perception on meeting each of the young men for the third time was that they had all grown in self-confidence and were more assertive; it did not matter which university they had attended, what class of degree they were hoping to achieve, or how advanced they were with their plans for the following year. They were engaged during the interview, offering open and frank insights into their lives. Many of them suggested keeping in touch. When, at the end of the interview, I thanked Edward, his response was: 'No! Thank you very much! It was nice to have someone ask about me. No one has ever done that. That's wicked.'

Table 5.1 acts as an aide memoire to show the type of university each participant attended, their proposed educational qualifications, and their career ambitions.

Table 5.1: Name, type of university, higher education qualification, career ambitions

Name	Type of university	Proposed further qualification	Career ambitions	Anticipated degree class
Adam	Elite	Master's	Engineering consultancy	2:1
Ben	Elite	Postgraduate	Solicitor	2:1
Craig	Elite	Teach First	History teacher	First/2:1
Graham	Elite	Undecided	Astronaut or PhD	First

Name	Type of university	Proposed further qualification	Career ambitions	Anticipated degree class
Ian	Elite	Undecided	Computer programming consultancy or postgraduate study (master's)	First
John	Elite	No further qualification	Undecided, possibly civil service or consultancy	First
Leon	Elite	Master's	Librarian	First
David	Modern	No further qualification	Football coaching	2:2
Edward	Modern	No further qualification	Football coaching	2:2
Frank	Modern	PGCE	PE teacher	2:1
Harvey	Modern	No further qualification	Football coaching or PE teacher	2:1/2:2
Karl	Modern	Master's	Education section of a museum	2:1
Mark	Modern	PGCE	PE teacher	First
Nathan	Modern	Dropped out in third year	Unknown	N/A
Oliver	Modern	Dropped out in second year	Unknown	N/A

A degree ... almost ...

When the third interview was conducted, the young men at the elite universities were very focused on their studies as they were all facing the prospect of upcoming exams. They were confident of passing, their main concern being whether they would be getting a first-class or upper second-class degree. Graham (physics) and Adam (engineering) were both undertaking four-year courses, but nonetheless had exams to prepare for. Of the others, Ben was: 'Hoping that I'll get a high 2:1'; Ian was: 'Aiming for a first this year'. Leon, too, said: 'I think I could get a first', as did John: 'I am still aiming for a first, which I think is entirely do-able.' Craig said that his tutors were telling him to:

> Go for firsts, go for firsts, and it is like of course I'm going to try
> but there is no mark scheme, no one tells you how to get a first,
> there is no mark scheme, there is no indication on how to get
> a first ... I don't even know, no one knows what gets a first ... I
> genuinely don't know how to do it and it is pure luck as far as I
> can see when I've written a good essay and when I've written a
> bad essay.

Craig was very frustrated with what he saw as the lack of transparency in the college assessment system and was adamant that if he did get a first it would be due more to luck than hard work.

The young men at the modern universities did not have exams to prepare for, but each had a thesis to write as well as an essay for each unit of study being undertaken. When asked what mark they thought they would attain, Edward, David, and Harvey said they were aiming for and hopeful of attaining a 2:2. However, Mark said: 'If I get to grips with my dissertation, the other subjects I'm quite competent in and confident about so I could go towards a low first if I put my head to it', and Karl confidently said: 'I won't get any lower than a 2:2 but I'm hoping for a 2:1.' Frank, too, was hoping for a 2:1 as this was what he needed to be considered for the PGCE programme. The young men had come to know the academic field and habitus; they understood that a third-class degree was no longer sufficient, and that a second-class degree was a minimum requirement in the job and postgraduate market.

The participants were (at the time of the last interview) very close to obtaining their bachelor's degrees, but it was not plain sailing for them. Frank had split his third year, which meant that he would take two years to complete his third year of study and would therefore not graduate until July 2015. David was yet to obtain ethical approval for his dissertation research; he also had yet to begin any work on the project, which was due in four weeks after our interview. He said that he had also not done any work towards the essays and folios due in the following month. He told me that:

> So yeah I'm struggling a bit ... it's a bit stressful because I just
> feel guilty because I haven't done it and that but it will be
> disappointing if I've got this far and then I mess it up yeah ...

When I asked him why this had occurred, his response was: 'I don't know why it's so bad this semester, probably because I haven't really gone in [to university] so I haven't got into the swing of things.' On further questioning, it transpired that David had met a young woman a few months previously and was spending a lot of time with her. He was not at all confident that he would meet his deadlines and graduate. He was in a precarious position, facing academic failure, something both he and his parents were keen for him to avoid. This had resulted in David 'kind of feeling guilty' because he felt he was letting his parents down if he did not graduate. Several of the young men found the road to obtaining a degree littered with obstacles; even, as David discovered, at the last hurdle there is 'a risk ... one thing or the other, it's like two paths'.

The changes undergone

When asked if they had changed during their three years at university, all believed they had. Only one participant, John, expressed the change negatively:

> I think I am a lot *less* confident now as a result ... I mean, in
> terms of my work, I mean the Oxbridge system seems to be based
> around doing the work then being told, them telling you why
> you are wrong, as opposed to teaching you and then trying. So I
> find it very difficult ... it feels that at all times you are constantly
> under-achieving.

This young man was in line to achieve a first-class degree but he had experienced some emotional problems along the way and socially did not feel he had learned to fit in:

> Like I don't have the common experiences, I don't even know the
> same sort of shops and I'm not as comfortable in coffee shops [as
> the other students] and things like that.

John continued to feel isolated within the institutional habitus of the university and after three years he was still floundering. John remained, in his own eyes, a 'cultural outsider' (Granfield, 1991). He felt out of place because he lacked the values and experiences of his middle-class counterparts. John was experiencing conflict that was caused because his habitus did not match the social field of his university (Bourdieu and Wacquant, 1992). While he had experienced significant academic success, he remained an outsider in a middle-class environment – he was a 'stranger in paradise' (Ryan and Sackrey, 1984).

One young man studying at a modern university, Karl, replied 'not massively' when asked if he had changed. However, later in the interview he acknowledged that:

It's opened me up to quite a few other options that I can do because originally I did come in looking to do teaching and decided against that. Yes, so it has helped me to see there are other things available.

Karl had lived at home while attending university, socializing only with home friends. He said that had he lived on campus:

My social life would probably be slightly different, because I would be going places which would be more campus orientated and stuff like that. Probably would've met a fair more number of people as well.

Clayton *et al.* (2009) suggest that, by living at home, some working-class students avoid the social milieu of university, thereby minimizing their social anxieties. This may well have been the case with Karl, who attended university only for lectures, not taking part in social events or getting involved with any clubs or societies. In fact, Karl could not even tell me what anyone else on his course was planning to do career-wise. He appeared to have had minimum levels of engagement with higher education and did not feel the need, or perhaps did not want, to fit in to university life, retaining his home-based friendships throughout his three years at university. Attending university, for Karl, was almost no different from going to school and it did not seem to occur to him that he could participate in non-academic activities there. Karl had a functional relationship with the university, which he saw as a means to an end, the end being a second-class undergraduate degree (Holdsworth, 2006).

All of the other young men considered that they had changed quite significantly. They had adapted their habituses. This adaptation had been noticed by family and friends. Harvey (modern) said that his vocabulary had changed: 'I would say that I've got quite a broad-range vocabulary and people at home they just don't know what it means and I'm like sorry I forgot.' Ian (elite) said:

When I go back home I have to change how I speak definitely because I have a much posher accent here than I do at home. And I get told off by my family a lot if I don't ... also the tone of the conversation changes a lot. Like I have to change a lot of vocabulary and the actual subject of things.

The cultural and social capital that Ian and Harvey had acquired while at university had changed their relationships with their families. They found themselves having to adopt two different identities: a working-class identity at home, which included a certain accent, vocabulary, and subject matter, and a more educated identity at university. All of the young men found some disjuncture between the two fields, but they also displayed the ability to successfully move across the fields.

This was particularly apparent for those attending elite universities, as Craig observed:

> Of course university opens up a wide range of ideas and people and that leads you in a very different direction ... we have very in-depth discussions, and that is what I like. You know I'm an academic and an intellectual at heart and I think I would find it very, very difficult to engage back. I have tried but you are just operating on two levels and it is horrible ... you just move in totally different spheres and it is a horrible, horrible concept to think.

Craig was feeling guilty as he reflected on and tried to come to terms with having left his old world behind. He believed that the changes he had undergone at university had led to some differences in ideological beliefs between himself and his family: 'My parents can look at me like "what are you on about?" Maybe being at university has made me a little more left wing ... and so we come in conflict.'

Craig felt the changes acutely and while he was very positive about how he had changed, and the cultural capital he had accumulated, he had not entirely come to terms with simultaneously inhabiting two different and conflicting worlds: the home world of working-class life and his newly developing educated world. He appeared to be experiencing a dislocation between his old habitus and his newly developed habitus, and with this came some anxiety and guilt (Baxter and Britton, 2001). Craig said: 'You do not have the social capital [in a working-class family], I do think it is a social and cultural thing.'

The *perceived* costs and the benefits of a university degree

Costs

The young men were asked if there had been any emotional, social, and/or economic costs in attending university. Ian's (elite) response was:

I don't really feel that I have lost anything by coming here. I can't imagine, maybe there would have been some people who would have preferred me before I had gone to uni, just in the sense that I talk slightly different now and my humour is going to be different. I don't feel I've noticed any potential loss.

Several other young men, like Ian, felt that there had been no costs to them in going to university; they included Edward (modern), Karl (modern), Ben (elite), and Graham (elite). Some felt there were minimal costs: David (modern) saw the costs in terms of financial and social loss: 'Not seeing old friends'. Mark (modern) had similar thoughts:

Well, financially I think there's been a lot ... I don't tend to see my friends a lot now. I don't keep in contact as much as I used to because it's hard when you are in London and they're all in [names home town] you feel a little bit left out.

Harvey (modern) also thought of the costs mainly in social terms, including the probability of losing home friends. Adam (elite) expressed the costs in emotional terms:

I guess when I talk to people from home or something you'll quite often get like a negative connotation for being at Oxbridge. Everyone's like 'ah you're at Oxbridge'. I didn't like telling people that I was even here.

Craig (elite) described the costs to himself in terms of moving in a completely different sphere from those at home. He explained that his mother seemed intimidated by the prospect of meeting people from the university. As he said:

She feels threatened by it, so whenever she comes up here we won't meet in college, it is always outside, she won't mix with anyone else. So it is interesting and it is a point where two worlds collide almost.

Leon (elite) was vague about the costs: 'There have been costs in that there have been sort of day-to-day costs, but I think no, I think on a wider level there haven't been.'

John (elite) expressed the costs in terms of having chosen an elite university in which to study. He had health problems, which he attributed to the academic pressure he encountered at university and he had not participated in any of the extracurricular activities on offer, choosing instead to concentrate solely on his academic work. He therefore did not mix socially with the other students.

After three years at university, John was still ill at ease. He was experiencing 'learning shock', which included acute frustration, confusion, and anxiety (Griffiths *et al.*, 2005). He had been unable to accrue and employ dominant forms of cultural and social capital and his university experience had been defined by the struggles he had faced.

Craig found the method of teaching frustrated him and, after three years at university, he still wrestled with it:

> It's a lot more work than other places judging by what my friends do [at other universities]. It is quite frustrating the way they teach you, it's probably going to knock your confidence but intentionally. It feels intentional. I mean why would you structure the workload to make you wrong and *then* tell you *why* you are wrong? You know there will be specific problems that they give us where it's literally no way we can figure it out because it's not in any text book, it's not in lectures, it's some trick they want us to figure out by ourselves ... and then you go to class ... and everyone will be wrong and then they will tell you why you are wrong.

The central theme that emerged from the narratives of those who felt there had been costs associated with attending university was one of social disjuncture, the fear of losing contact with family and friends. Although the changes they had undergone could be expressed in terms of social mobility, all had maintained strong links with their families.

Benefits

The young men attending elite universities understood the benefits mainly in terms of career prospects, though many enjoyed other advantages, as Ian told me:

> It is not so much the academics but where will I be able to, on a Saturday, go and play some ultimate frisbee and then on Sunday go and play quidditch and then on Monday just go dancing. It is not realistic to do that anywhere else.

He went on to say that at university 'you mix with a broad range of people' and:

The subjects of conversation are so different it just changes how you see everything because before everything was in what felt like a smaller, much smaller bubble than what there is here.

Adam, too, could see all kinds of benefits:

You're pushed a lot ... I think you develop skills that you wouldn't develop elsewhere because you are under ... immense time pressure, there's a lot you have got to do ... The opportunities just from being here are great, like there are so many events, so many things to get involved with that you can always find new things to do ... you always find new people to chat to ... and it basically is a massive networking opportunity.

These young men understood the advantages of attending an elite university, not only in academic terms but also in social terms, and they had succeeded in managing any disjuncture between habitus and field. Their reflexive habituses and highly developed academic natures generated academic success and opportunities.

The young men attending the modern universities, while generally not as effusive about the benefits of going to university, were nevertheless positive about the advantages a university degree confers. Harvey said:

I've become more independent, which is always a good thing ... I see myself getting a better job than what they've [his friends] got, let me put it that way, and, I think they know that as well, that's why they know I've gone to uni and stuff. So I just feel like coming to uni has made like, made me more intelligent than I already was so I can get a better job like when you go for a job interview saying I've got a degree.

Harvey went on to say that having a degree would enable him to have a career such as PE teaching or football coaching, which he would enjoy, whereas his friends were in jobs they did not enjoy. Karl saw that university had, for him, opened up options that he had not considered before going to university. Edward, too, felt that university had broadened his horizons:

Going to uni helps you because [you meet] people who go travelling ... and you talk to more people ... I want to explore the planet and explore all these different things.

Mark saw the benefits of university in employment terms:

> I've got more chance of getting a successful job ... you can't do anything without qualifications unless you want to be a labourer or something like that.

Frank, the only young man at a modern university who had remained in university accommodation for the entire duration of his studies, was very effusive about the advantages of attending university:

> University brings this whole new thing ... you experience different things, you experience different people, you come out of your comfort zone ... [it] made me more understanding of other people.

Frank had become friendly not only with fellow students but with members of staff as well: 'Because it can help, it really can, it can open doors to opportunities that might not be there for other people.' He had taken the opportunities offered at university to acquire and develop an understanding of the benefits of connections in this competitive world of career building.

All of the young men, even those who were not sure about where they were heading, had come to university to secure employment in higher-status jobs/careers than their parents. The transformation of their working-class habitus through education was seen by them and their parents as the route to what they perceived as better employment prospects.

Future plans and career ambitions

All but one of the young men who had attended the modern universities had come either through a BTEC route or an access course, whereas all of those at the elite universities had A level qualifications. The latter were focused on pursuing their career choices immediately on completing their degrees or postgraduate degrees and to this end had, in most cases, secured employment before they had completed their studies. On the other hand, of those attending the modern universities, only one (Edward) appeared to have applied for any form of employment and none had, at the time of the last interview, secured employment.

Modern universities and career opportunities

Karl was the only participant to have studied education. He thought that he would obtain a 2:1 and he had a very clear picture of the career he wished to pursue – to work in the education section of a museum. At the time of our last interview, however, he had yet to apply for any positions, though he confidently stated that he was planning 'to start applying in the next couple of months'. When asked what he would do if he did not get a job in his chosen field, he responded: 'I guess I will do what most people do, just sign on and keep trying.' Karl explained that, as he saw it: 'The problem with the job market [is that], everyone [employers] wants experience but there's no one giving experience.' He had volunteered to work part time in a charity shop to gain retail experience in the hope that this would increase his job prospects. He was not troubled by a potential lack of employment, as he had a plan of sorts and he continued to live at home.

Frank had split the third year of his degree, so was planning to go back to university to complete his third year in the academic year 2014/15. Four of the young men who had attended modern universities expressed a desire to travel and this had not always been met with enthusiasm by their parents. Mark had been offered a teaching assistant (TA) position at his former secondary school. When I questioned why he had not accepted the position, he responded: 'Well it's just I would like to go travelling.' Mark's parents were very keen for him to accept the TA position and suggested that he travel in the summer and take the TA job, which began in the September following graduation. Beyond this, Mark was keen to pursue a teaching career and wanted to do a PGCE at some point in the future. At the time of the final interview, Mark had yet to decide on any plans beyond university, although he was planning to live at home.

David also had plans to travel after completing his sports science degree, as he explained: 'I just want to relax for the next kind of few years after uni, do a bit of travel.' He did go on to say that he had been offered a part-time coaching position for a year at one of the schools in which he had been on placement, but, like Mark, had not taken up the offer. David was planning to live in a flat with some school friends who were also completing their studies at university.

When I enquired of Edward what his plans were post-university, he responded:

> I tell you what I'm going to do for at least two weeks, from two weeks to a month, there's a game called Football Manager, a PC game ... so on the day I finish, April 28th, I will have that game and I will not be leaving my house for two weeks.

He added: 'I want to travel as well as do football coaching.' Edward appeared to be the only young man at a modern university who had sent off his CV to any organization:

> I've applied for and sent CVs off for a lot of jobs across the world really, like abroad, to America and Asia and South America and stuff and a few obviously in the UK. But I mean I have no idea where I would, I probably should have my next job in the UK just so I can save up, because obviously, I want to go travelling ... but I wouldn't rule out anything, if there was a job turned up in Dubai for instance or South Korea I wouldn't turn it down.

Edward continued to live at home and he, like Mark and David, had a part-time fall-back job if other employment failed to materialize:

> The coaching job I was doing before Christmas, he [Edward's employer] said, 'when you finish your degree you can have it back' kind of thing so that's nice to hear and the pay's good and it's a sporty job.

Harvey, like Mark, was feeling the pressure from his parents:

> Like they keep harassing me and they're like what you going to do and my mum's like let's talk about it. I need to pass uni first, I need to focus on that and then I don't know. I said to them last year that I want to go to like America or Australia and do some football coaching there ... like there's plenty of websites that I've looked into and that and it's just like moving away for like six months ... I don't know if my mum would let me move for six months.

Harvey had the offer of a coaching job with the Arsenal soccer schools, which he could do in the summer holidays if he wished, and, when pushed about what his plans were longer term, he responded with:

> Come September I'm not really sure ... I think I'm just taking it as it comes. I'm not one of them people to plan that far ahead. Like, if something comes up then yeah that's what I would do but if nothing does come up then I think I will start looking around maybe for more coaching jobs like maybe like full-time coaching jobs rather than just term time. Or maybe Arsenal, ask Arsenal whether I can, if they've got more hours to work full-time, maybe I can be pushed up into that bracket or something ... but that will be the sort of time where I'd have to just decide whether I could pursue football coaching as a career or whether I should start setting up my personal statement for the PGCE for the following year and then go for interviews if I get accepted and stuff like

that. But I think that's the sort of two avenues that I'm going down, either teaching or coaching, because I think that's the two things that I'd most enjoy.

The young men who completed their sports science degree all left academia, at least in the short term, and while their longer-term plans did not seem well formulated, they did all have jobs, albeit part-time ones, to fall back on.

The degree course they had chosen dictated the type of work they planned to undertake. These young men (although Frank was an outlier here) retained close links to their homes and localities while at university. Career ambitions for them were very much football-focused. They had played football/rugby at university and/or for clubs outside the university. One young man played football semi-professionally. They had earned what Bourdieu (1978) refers to as 'physical capital': their love of, and ability to play, football/rugby influenced their choice to study for a BTEC in sport in the sixth form. Having done well in these studies, they chose to attend university. They had achieved academic success by channelling this 'physical capital' into 'academic capital' and were aiming to convert their 'academic capital' into 'economic capital'.

Elite universities and career opportunities

At the time of the last interview, John was the only participant who was yet to focus on future career opportunities and he said that his parents were concerned about this: 'But they are quite happy for me to be as I am, just trying to do as well as I can in my degree before I move on.' When I asked John what his plans were once he had completed his last exam, he responded:

> Leave [named the university] as soon as possible. Probably go home and then hopefully forget about this ever happening and start applying for jobs somewhere so I cannot be a burden on my family and move out essentially.

Each time I interviewed John, he was to a lesser or greater degree experiencing anxieties, self-doubts, and disappointments. He remained isolated as he was unable to build friendships with his peers (Griffiths *et al.*, 2005). John was hoping that once he left the confines of the university environment, he would return to some semblance of what he considered normality and begin the next stage of his life, that of considering a career. He believed that by returning to a place (home) in which he felt more comfortable, things would improve for him.

The other young men had much clearer career plans. Graham had been shortlisted for an astronaut training programme and, if chosen, he planned to do that; but if he wasn't chosen, he planned to do a PhD in astrophysics and become an academic. Ben, who was completing a law degree, had accepted a training contract with a leading London law firm.

Craig had accepted a place with Teach First (an elite postgraduate teacher education course) to teach history and English. He said that when he told his step-father this, his step-father had 'pooh-poohed that I haven't taken on something that is perhaps a little bit more higher salary'. But Craig went on to say that: 'Teach First is quite good at opening avenues.' He understood that the Teach First programme could lead to other career opportunities for him in the future.

Ian informed me that he had applied for a position with a few companies as a computer science consultant. He said that if he was offered a job that appealed to him, he would take it, but otherwise he would stay on and undertake a master's degree before embarking on a career. When I asked Ian why he had chosen to apply for the positions that he had, he responded that he had received advice at a computer science careers fair held at university. He had also searched a database of the top 100 graduate employers.

Leon had been accepted to do a Master of Arts (MA) programme at another university and was then planning to do a librarian traineeship. Adam, who was studying engineering and had a fourth year to complete, said that he was undertaking a placement with a major international consultancy group in his summer holidays. This placement, he said, might lead to the offer of employment on graduation.

Except for John, all of the young men at elite universities had adapted to the academic field. They had learned the 'rules of the game' and had even acquired 'trump cards' and good-quality capital (Bourdieu and Wacquant, 1992). They were now moving on to careers appropriate to their soon-to-be-acquired academic qualifications. They all understood the value of having been at an elite university. Even John told me he would make the same choice again:

> Because the reasons for coming here haven't changed too much. It's still going to be hard work but it's the *label*, it's three years versus 50 years you know. It's a trade-off I'm willing to make.

When I asked Adam what career plans his friends from university had, he told me: 'Friends from here are sorted.' He mentioned a list of employers:

leading law, accounting, and consultancy firms as well as major banks. These young men fully understood that the 'best companies' distinguished between their universities and others and that these companies wanted the 'brightest' students working for them (Brown and Hesketh, 2004).

Withdrawals

It is well documented that men from poorer backgrounds are less likely to attend university than those from other backgrounds, but what is less well known is that men from this cohort who do attend university are also less likely to complete a degree (Quinn, 2013). There are also variations in average continuation rates between the different types of university, with the elite universities having the highest continuation rates and the modern universities having the lowest (NAO, 2007). Figures for 2014/15 from the Social Market Foundation (2016) show that, on average, the elite universities had a withdrawal rate of 1.2 per cent and the modern universities had a withdrawal rate of 9.4 per cent.

Variation in withdrawal rates by entry qualification is substantial. Withdrawal rates for students who enter university with at least three As at A level was 1.9 per cent, while those with three Cs at A level had a withdrawal rate of 4.5 per cent. Access course students had an average withdrawal rate of 15.6 per cent and those entering with a BTEC had an average withdrawal rate of 12.7 per cent, according to the Higher Education Funding Council for England (HEFCE, 2013).

Yorke and Longden (2004) explored the possible reasons for these variations and found that students who felt they had chosen the wrong course were more likely to withdraw from university. Working full time was also a factor in early withdrawal, whereas there was no difference in withdrawal rates between students who worked short part-time hours or did no work. Lehmann (2007), in his study on university withdrawal rates, found that middle-class students withdrew as a last resort and usually because of academic failure, whereas most first-generation working-class students left voluntarily and for non-academic reasons.

Two participants withdrew from university during my study, and while I have been unable to follow up with either of them, I did conduct one interview with Oliver and two with Nathan. In these interviews, I established that Nathan had come to university with a BTEC qualification and Oliver had undertaken A levels and achieved two Cs and a D. From the figures presented earlier, it is clear to see that with these levels of qualifications the two young men's chances of withdrawing from university were substantially higher than for those who achieved three As at A level.

Oliver told me that he found his current course undemanding. He had originally enrolled in, and completed, 18 months of the Qualified Teacher Status (QTS) programme but voluntarily withdrew because he had experienced substantial trauma in his private life. On returning to university the following year, he discovered that the QTS programme had been discontinued and he found himself on a course that was very much a second choice. He described the original course he was on as:

> Fantastic! It was interesting but hard work and kept you busy whereas this one, I will end up with a piece of paper that says I've got a degree but ...

Oliver was also working full time as a bar manager, which involved much late-night work.

In my last interview with Nathan, he said that he was finding it difficult to remain motivated and this was problematic for him: 'I've only had two modules, so four hours a week, which is a struggle to keep yourself entertained sometimes.' Perhaps the university experience was not what they expected, and/or in Oliver's case the need to work for economic reasons made full-time study untenable. Whatever the reasons, they withdrew from university by choice and not for academic reasons.

Discussion

This section examines the role played by dominant cultures of masculinity and any influences that aspects of these discourses may have played in the academic progress of my participants.

Many of those who had attended elite universities had been marginalized at school for not being sporty and for adopting an academic persona. They had been 'othered' for not adopting some of the anti-school, pro-sport cultures that were in circulation. Craig referred to being called a 'geek', as did others. At university, they discovered a culture that was academically focused and where doing well was in the ascendancy. Even John who was still an 'outsider', recognized the dominance of this pro-work, pro-success regime. What these findings suggest is that cultures of masculinity may be changing and that different contexts produce their own cultures.

The young men who studied sports science were, as argued in Chapter 4, caught up in a sports-masculinity discourse through their participation in football/rugby while simultaneously maintaining their commitment to academic study. They converted their 'sporting capital' into 'academic capital' and were planning to convert this into 'economic capital'. They had drawn on contemporary versions of masculinity that are perhaps more complex and nuanced than older versions suggest (Gee, 2014).

Having completed the interviews and 'watched' these young men develop over their time at university, seeing them eager to get on with the rest of their lives reminded me of the subtitle of a book written in 1997 by Bynner *et al.*: 'Getting on, getting by, getting nowhere'. While I did not get the impression that any of the young men I interviewed were 'getting nowhere', I did feel that some of them were going to be *getting by*' in the job market. As David put it: 'Job wise I think probably just be something to get by ... a teaching assistant ... like I haven't really started something.' In the final interview, some of them said that they would concentrate on getting work once they had left university. Thinking about and looking for employment was almost an afterthought for some of them.

Those young men looking to be football coaches, or just looking for a job that would 'get them by', would be entering a job market offering mainly part-time work with no job security and limited prospects of career development and advancement. On the other hand, those going to leading City law firms and consultancy firms had been considering their career options since the second year of university. They did internships or placements in their summer holidays in the tacit understanding that this would be good for their future career. By the end of the third year, they were very focused on obtaining employment in occupations commensurate with their academic qualifications. University had provided these young men with the opportunities to acquire the cultural capital to enable them to confidently 'get on'.

The young men who achieved As and A*s at A level and went on to attend elite universities were going to fill the ranks of the professions. Those who achieved BTEC qualifications and then entered modern universities found that their career opportunities were limited to sports coaching, sports teaching, and the leisure industry. This could limit their remuneration level (Bynner *et al.*, 1997).

Green and Zhu (2010) argue that we have reached the point where some university graduates are underemployed in jobs that make little use of their university qualifications. Indeed, many recent graduates take up positions in the labour market that do not require degrees, although the possession of a degree signals that the employee has some transferable skills.

The Office for National Statistics reported that in 2013, 47 per cent of university graduates were in non-graduate employment (2013). With unprecedented numbers now entering the workforce with a bachelor's degree, the price of educated labour has reduced. A growing number of aspiring working-class families are becoming disappointed as they have failed to understand that, although a bachelor's degree from the best universities still confers the best employment benefits, this is not the situation for all undergraduate degrees (Brown, 2013).

Whether these findings are reflected in the experiences of the young men in this study is yet to be seen. Certainly, those who attended elite universities have secured employment in fields considered commensurate with their qualifications; and those who attended modern universities all believed that their university qualifications would hold them in good stead in the marketplace. There is consensus that the possession of any degree is still a useful indicator of capacity to learn and aspiration to succeed. Thus, graduates still have an employability 'bonus' compared with non-graduates (Burke, 2016).

It is well known that some universities in England are better resourced than others (Crozier *et al.*, 2008; Callender and Scott, 2013), with the better resourced usually being the higher-status universities. My sample includes both funding extremes, with the elite providers having the resources necessary to provide students with personally focused learning experiences that are in shorter supply in the newer universities.

The young men who attended elite universities were provided with some highly individualized learning experiences and were assisted in finding work experience in professional organizations where they were often offered full-time employment on graduation. It is well known that those attending elite universities are more likely to pursue a professional career, while 40 per cent of those attending new universities pursue managerial posts (Sutton Trust, 2014).

Some of the young men who attended modern universities were hoping to pursue teaching careers, while others were interested in managerial roles in the sports and leisure industry. They all understood that the subjects they had studied would shape their career choices to some extent, but they did not see this as a limitation. From their perspectives, they were going to seek employment in a field with which they were familiar, and one that they enjoyed.

I conclude this chapter by reiterating that all of the young men reported benefiting from their university experiences. They had all become more confident and, in terms of the Bourdieusian concepts I used to frame my research, they had extended their social capital, transformed their habituses, and were confident about their transition from university to the world of work.

Chapter 6

Why white working-class males do not engage academically

Class matters because it creates unequal possibilities for flourishing and suffering.

(Sayer, 2009: 218)

A sense of disenfranchisement

The young men I interviewed experienced academic success, but this is not the norm for most white working-class young men. This chapter explores this phenomenon from the perspective of the participants. They were asked what they saw as the cause of the under-achievement of many of their peers and what they thought could make an educational difference. Their explanations were often constructed with reference to themselves and their experiences of family and school life.

Family habitus

All of the participants raised the importance of the family and particularly the role of parents in encouraging educational success in their offspring. They recognized that habitus plays a central role in influencing educational outcomes. In what they said, it was possible to trace Bourdieu's claims about the primary habitus of the home and its role in establishing sets of conscious and unconscious practices (Bourdieu and Wacquant, 1992). For example, Karl believed that white working-class males' lack of engagement with education emanated, in part, from a lack of social capital on the part of some working-class parents, who did not always know enough about the education system to be able to advise their children:

> Rather than just looking at boys in general, you should take a more in-depth look at their social background because that has a big impact on who they are.

Ian suggested that white working-class males' under-achievement was, in part, due to a lack of motivation on the part of the boys themselves. He felt that boys needed 'to get that motivation from someone in a position of authority ... your parents ... encouraging you'. Ian raised this issue in two of the three interviews, saying: 'I think it is kind of firstly a lack of enthusiasm from the parents about it [education].' Mark, too, thought that parental encouragement was crucial and, without it, young people failed to engage with education. Oliver agreed: 'I would say that the main thing would be what your parents are like, whether they encourage you to do well from a young age.' Harvey said that his mother was the driving force behind his continuing education: 'She can see in 20 years' time ... if you go and do this then the benefits for you are going to be much higher.' He observed that a lot of young men do not have this level of parental support and 'like they don't think it's [education] for them'.

Leon reasoned that parents who had left school at the statutory age were less likely to value education and 'pass that down to their children'. However, Karl thought that the encouragement to go on to further and higher education came from both the home and the school.

Cultures of masculinity – doing what dad does

Dominant forms of masculinity are often referred to in the research on the failure of young white males to engage with education (Smith, 2007). Several young men said that many of their cohort treated school and education with disdain, leaving school as soon as they legally could. Mark said that some white working-class boys took education 'for granted and think it is something I've got to do and then rebel against it'. Nathan explained that: 'Lots of kids were dying to get out of school at 16 and by the time they have done their GCSEs, they couldn't wait to leave, to have freedom.' Graham's answer was reflexive:

> I think the problem is with the school system, that it doesn't help
> you identify what's the thing you enjoy doing and what you want
> to go on and do. And lots of people just get fed up in lessons and
> decide they want to go and earn some money or something and
> because of that there is an urgency to get out of school.

Another claim made by my participants was that white working-class young men traditionally follow their fathers. Oliver described it as: 'Dad sort of knows what he is talking about with money so, I just like, follow that kind of thing and not go to university.' Edward had school friends who thought:

> They'd go into their dads' job when they were 16 ... I just think it
> is usually their parents have jobs like in the trades and stuff and
> they get jobs from it. It is easy for their dad to give them a job and

they just get used to it and bosh, they are in a full-time job. A lot of examples from my mates at school, their dads own a company or electrical whatever, and they just go into it just because their dad owns it.

Leon commented: 'Where I was brought up was quite a rural and agricultural area, a lot of kids and dads were farmers.' Leon went on to say that some of the white working-class boys he was at school with did reasonably well academically but did not consider higher education because: 'Their parents had always worked manually and they just didn't know anything different.' This view was echoed by Adam, who told me that most of the young people in his school had parents in vocational jobs so that was their plan. David told me that one of his friends 'is working in Marks & Spencer's waiting for his dad to die so he can take his business'.

Craig explained that, as he saw it, in the past 'it used to be acceptable for you as a white working-class boy to grow up and do the same job as your dad and that used to be a source of pride'. Craig was from a naval town and, previously, many of the working-class boys in this area were employed at 16 in industries involved in ship building:

If you weren't on the ship, you were making the ships and if you weren't making the ships you were controlling the ships ... But now we are in this curious transition period where that idea of you just go and do what your father did is not there.

Craig pointed out that the ship-building industry in his area no longer exists and the employment that it provided has disappeared; and the navy has contracted, so jobs have been shed there also. Hence the employment opportunities for white working-class young men with limited academic qualifications have shrunk considerably in Craig's town. He went on to say: 'There is no established tradition of going into academia for working-class boys because they always did what their dad did', so they often do not consider university as an option.

David told me that, in his view, some fathers of white working-class boys often see education as unnecessary:

I think if they are white working-class, and their dad's like a sparky or something, they'd probably get it in the ear all the time about how it's [education] useless and how you might as well just go out and get a job and start earning money.

According to Jones (2012), for most white working-class young men, education does not seem to be even remotely relevant to their lives.

The home environment and comfort zone

David explained that some of the young men he knew did do reasonably well academically, but they chose not to go to university because:

> They are so sheltered they don't want to live on their own, they don't want to go into an environment that is unsettling, they just want to stay in their own environment and comfort zone ... It is just like their comfort zone. They don't want to go through change ... so I think it is more kind of like their attitude.

Adam, who came from a mining town, said: 'People don't really move away from my area. Once you are there you are there.' Craig, too, referred to this attachment to the familiar:

> Everyone knows everyone, it is very incestuous, everyone has gone to the same school that their parents have gone to and has done the same things. Everyone supports [names football team], there is still very much that cohesion.

He went on to say that many people stay in the town even if they cannot find work. He used his brother as an example: 'He wants to move out but I don't know if he will ... He resigns himself to it because that is what his friends are doing.'

People from a white working-class background are very strongly attached to the familiar, to their locality, to the space they know, as well as to friends and family. Many working-class people find it difficult to be separated from locality (Archer *et al.*, 2010).

When Frank told his mother that he wanted to go to university, he told me that she had responded: 'Look, if you don't really want to, no one is going to think any different of you, okay?' but that: 'I was like no, I want to go to university.' His mother then wanted him to pick a university close to the family, so one of the universities he put on his UCAS application was 'because it was close to home and it kept Mum's mind at bay because she knew I'd be kind of close to her'. Interestingly, the university that Frank is attending is quite some distance (200 miles) from his family home and he explained that he was 'kind of glad I picked [named university] because it is far enough away but I can still go back'. Frank also commented that his sister had not wanted him to go to university and his mother had been very concerned that he was so far from home.

This concept that the working classes navigate the space that is familiar to them, and often remain within a familiar space, has been developed by Appadurai (2004). He suggests that the better off in society are in a better position to explore diverse experiences and transcend the limits of the local. They have used the map of society's norms to navigate and explore these experiences, sharing this knowledge with one another more routinely than their less well-off neighbours. These better-off members of a society can navigate the complex steps between aspirations and outcomes more easily than those who are less well off. The less well off have a more brittle horizon and set of aspirations simply because they have limited opportunities and capacity to travel beyond the boundaries of their neighbourhood to explore diverse opportunities.

The young men in my study developed their navigational skills, thereby expanding their horizons. However, most of their friends from home remained attached to the familiar, navigating in social and economic terms within the space that was familiar, living and working there.

Teachers and schools
Raising aspirations
Other factors raised by the young men when discussing why they think white working-class young males tend to do less well educationally were related to the role of the teachers, the school, and the educational process. The quality of teachers' relationships with students was found by Dunne and Gazeley (2008) to be an important factor in student learning, as were the provision of engaging activities for students and listening to what they had to say about their learning. These themes also came through in my interviews.

For instance, Craig thought that schools could do more to 'nurture most simply the intellect and provide more experiences for working-class students such as trips to museums, the theatre, and the like'. Ben suggested that good guidance from members of staff was important and that: 'Aspiring to traditionally successful paths could very much be encouraged by members of staff.' Ian suggested that, from Year 5 or 6, children be taught to understand the benefits of education because: 'It is really easy to get into the idea that school is something that you have to do and you just make your way through until it is finally over.' Adam, who came from a village with a population that was 99% white working class, said that over two-thirds of the students in his school left after GCSEs. He commented: 'I think our school accepts that its catchment area isn't the best' so the students 'were never pushed'.

Several of the young men claimed that schools accept that white working-class children will leave school at 16 with or without qualifications, a view confirmed by research conducted on teacher actions and assumptions about working-class academic performance. The failure of many working-class children to enter university is seen by many teachers not as a problem but rather as something to be expected (Dunne and Gazeley, 2008).

The study participants highlighted the importance of teachers, and saw what teachers did and what happened in classrooms as central to their academic performance. Their primary habitus of the home was transformed into a secondary habitus by their educational experience. They also understood that, while they had positive school-based experiences, this was not the lot of most of their white working-class peers.

Harvey, Graham, and Edward suggested that students should be informed by the school/teachers of the possibilities that are open to them if they do well academically. In the same vein, Adam thought that schools should inform their students of careers, such as those in financial services or in the law, 'that people from where I come from don't really have any experience with'. Graham suggested that it would be helpful if schools had:

> More external people coming into schools and telling them about what different careers and things are actually like. Yes, that is what is really missing; you are stuck in the school system and you don't really know where it ends. And what needs to happen, the reason you don't know how it ends, is because you get to choose how it ends, that isn't something that we [white working-class boys] understand. Yes, so it is about you and your choice, not about what the teachers say.

The young men explained that there was often a dearth of information on further and higher education options available to students from a white working-class background and they thought that schools could fill this gap. They were suggesting that schools could assist social mobility by extending their social capital to more of their students, and teachers should change their expectations that most students from a white working-class background would leave school on completing their compulsory education.

Research by Foskett *et al.* (2008) on the influence of the school on the decision to participate in learning post-16 found that the socio-economic status of the school's intake strongly shaped the ethos, aims, and *aspirations* of the school.

The participants, in a positive vein, suggested that if a school and its leadership encouraged post-16 education for all, this policy would become embedded in the ethos of the school, thereby becoming an aspiration for its students. This point was made by all of them.

Setting, categorizing, and labelling

Several of the young men spoke about the effects that they thought setting had on the aspirations of white working-class students. Ability-based grouping is a contentious issue within UK education, with researchers divided over the potential advantages and disadvantages of this practice. Some researchers suggest that high-ability students are 'held back' in mixed-ability classes and that these students are stretched when setting is in place (Loveless, 1999, cited in Hodgen, 2011). Other researchers assert that setting is the principal cause of under-achievement, arguing that lower-achievers receive a poorer educational experience in setted environments where movement between ability groups is limited, resulting in many students' educational path being determined at a very young age (Hallam and Parsons, 2013).

Several of the young men also suggested that being put in a lower set acted as an academic deterrent:

> I just think you have got to try and make it [schooling] more inclusive ... If you are in the lower set you obviously prime yourself that you are no good at it. So maybe they could abolish the sets and then have a mixture of sets and then use the smart people, well set the smart people to help the lower ones.
>
> (Harvey)

John raised the issue of sets and the negative effect it could have on some students:

> I think a lot of the time you got sorted into a lower set or something and it was like oh that's me done, I'm never going to be smart enough kind of situation ... they see it as people giving up on them more than anything.

According to John, students in lower sets understood that teachers did not see them as academically able and therefore had low expectations for them.

As stated by the young men, setting has an overall negative educational and social effect on those who find themselves in the lower sets. They repeatedly stated that they thought many white working-class young males were negatively affected if they were in the lower-ability groups at school.

Graham thought that some children may have had:

Some kind of initial disadvancement coming from home, for example. That then gets amplified by the school system ... It is about finding what they want to do and pointing them in the direction to do that ... Yes, school should be about supporting people on what they want to do.

Taking Graham's quote, perhaps we could postulate that a child goes to school with 'some kind of initial disadvancement' (disadvantage) such as coming from a low socio-economic background, being male, having a mother without educational qualifications, being raised in a one-parent family, having been born in the summer (and thus being younger than others in the school year), and not having been read to at home. If a child experiences these initial educational disadvantages, he may well find himself in the bottom set at school, because according to Hallam and Parsons (2013), the characteristics listed above are those that children in the bottom set often exhibit. These initial educational disadvantages are then amplified by the school system, because setting exacerbates rather than improves the problems.

Frank was critical of some teachers, suggesting: 'Some teachers aren't putting the work in; they are just saying: "Right you are a problem child, you'll go to one side" ... If the teachers don't help then the kids have no hope.' Could it be that 'problem children' are created in a setted school? Setting may also affect the quality of teaching and resources, which differ between the sets, with the better-qualified and experienced teachers teaching the top set as this is seen as the best use of the teachers' expertise in a performative culture.

In Chapter 1, a quote from David gave an overview of what the school experience can be like for some white working-class young men. David told this story in a very level-headed way. He was not blaming anyone and he was aware that this was very much from his perspective. David was the exception in his GCSE bottom-set class. The other young people in his class did not have any expectation of experiencing academic success and, from what David said, the teachers also had little expectation that those children in the lower set would experience academic success. Thus, it could be argued that the habitus of the school positions white working-class males as 'deficient' and as 'not academic', and this view underpins everything that takes place.

Ireson and Hallam (2009) found that students' academic self-concept was strongly related to the set they were in, with those in the lowest-ability set having a negative academic self-concept and those in the highest-ability set having a positive academic self-concept. In their survey of 1,500 teachers, they found that there were considerable differences in the teaching of low- and high-ability groups, even when the same teacher taught both groups. The children in the lower sets were taught a different curriculum in a different manner, with less discussion, less homework, less feedback, more practical work, and more repetition. It is sobering to note Hallam and Parsons' (2013) finding that more than half the children in the bottom set were defined as living in poverty.

I end this section with the message that: 'Teachers and schools *can* make a difference – by believing, and acting as if, all students have the potential to succeed' (Hodgen, 2011: 219) (my italics).

University as an option?

The young men suggested that for many white working-class young men, university is not considered an option. They said that the schools they attended did not have a university focus and it was not discussed by the teachers. A few had had school friends come and visit them at university and many of their visitors expressed surprise at what university was.

Adam told me that university:

> Is never really something that people think about ... like when my friends come to visit, like most of them say they wished they had applied to university ... just like [they] weren't genuinely aware that there were options to go to university ... people need to be encouraged, I guess yes, the school could encourage more people to apply to university.

Ben said that many teachers do not believe that their white working-class students have the potential to get into elite universities:

> If there are no members of staff who are actively encouraging their students to go for it, then students are just going to think 'no one from my school has ever gone to Oxbridge'.

He felt it was important to have individual staff members who encouraged young people to apply to elite universities 'and who are also dispelling the ridiculous myths that go around about this place'. Many of the young men expressed similar thoughts. They felt that, in many cases, the teachers at their schools did not, or could not, provide enough information about the best subjects to study if one wanted to attend university, about the different types of university – that is, modern, red-brick, or elite – the different academic requirements of the various types of university, and so on.

The Sutton Trust is aware of this deficit and runs Teacher Summer Schools each year. It targets teachers from schools that send relatively few students to leading universities and which are sited in areas of socio-economic challenge.

Some teachers are not providing white working-class students with a full knowledge of the options available to them on leaving school, including higher education options. Teachers can transform the primary habitus of their students by exposing them to aspects of cultural and social capital that would be useful in promoting the benefits of education beyond compulsory schooling and the possibilities that an extended education may bring. Even before they leave school, some young people who are considered to be less able are encouraged, according to Wolf (2011), to take courses that might contribute to school performance tables, but which may not actually benefit the students themselves. This can leave some students with no capacity to attend university because the subjects they have studied are not recognized by the universities.

Role models/mentors

The young men suggested that mentors and/or role models are critical for white working-class children because, often, parents do not have the cultural or social capital needed to make wider educational opportunities available to them. Graham thought that:

> There is the potential for a role model to be a powerful influence to most people ... Yes, I think people in general just need help to find what they want to do. Then they will be able to find their way themselves.

Leon suggested that:

> Every child has one individual person who makes them aware that they are really important and they can do really good things; you know that is the main thing.

For Harvey, it was 'all about that role model, maybe someone giving them a bit of leadership'. He suggested that young men from white working-class backgrounds who are currently at university could act as these role models:

> The youth of today they relate to the youth, peers, more than anything ... so if they see someone else taking the initiative to go off to uni then it will give them that little bit of motivation.

Ian said that, for him, having a teacher mentor who was prepared to challenge him was extremely beneficial:

> Just having the right teacher really helped me ... the maths teacher was really enthusiastic about maths ... he would give me something more challenging, more interesting ... So that like really helped and showed that some people can really enjoy it, instead of just having to do it, you can enjoy some academic things. I think that really helps.

This perspective is supported in the academic literature, which suggests that the role of a mentor can be important for the academic success of young men from a white working-class background (Spencer, 2007; Travers, 2011). Teacher mentors can provide academic stimulus, support, and guidance as well as non-academic support. The participants realized that key individuals could expose white working-class males to aspects of cultural and social capital that promote positive attitudes to education. Craig's comment highlights this:

> I would also say that white, working-class boys have been neglected. I don't know why that is but I never felt I had a role model and role models I think are important.

Lack of aspiration and a fear of failure

There appears to be a lack of academic aspiration among many white working-class males, which is seen as a deficiency on their part. However, the question of why they lack academic aspirations has been little explored. Is it because they find themselves unable to experience academic success and so they produce a 'self' that is valued in other ways? The students who are not academically successful may produce another self that could encompass being good at football, not putting any effort into academic study, being disruptive, or attacking those students who are academically successful. The young men said that this lack of aspiration is caused by several different factors, not all of them attributable to the young men themselves. Leon explained the lack of academic aspiration and under-achievement as a culture:

> There is a sort of masculine culture we have in the UK ... it is very important as a teenage boy to be into that and be part of

that and have friends and that involves under-achieving, sort of consciously, and doing other things with your time ... not to do well academically, it is important when you are a teenager to want to buy into the popular culture and have friends.

Graham also suggested: 'We have a kind of culture established where it is cool to be innumerate.' John shared this view: 'It was like a race to the bottom in terms of effort in the classroom ... I think the culture was very much against [school]work.'

These sentiments are similar to those expressed in the 1970s by the lads in Willis's ethnographic study on young working-class men and their transitions from school to work (Willis, 1977). The 'lads' referred to any young boys interested in academic study as 'ear'oles' whose academic success was discredited as lacking a robust masculinity. As the lads saw it, manual labour was for real men and academic study was socially inferior.

John thought many white working-class boys were resigned to their fate: 'I'm never going to have a chance to do it because I'm not smart enough.' Craig also referred to a sense of 'defeatism; a lack of ambition and sense of disenfranchisement: "I have no say, I have no control"'. He went on to say that some young white working-class males gave up on academic study 'way too quickly' and:

> Then it sort of drew all the people from my school into that sort of class of giving up ... in terms of effort there was a race to the bottom ... a sort of critical mass of people not caring.

According to Craig, for some young white working-class men, it was better not to try than to try and then fail:

> Yeah, it feels like there's a risk that they are not prepared to take in actually putting the effort in ... like if I don't revise and get a poor grade that's okay, if I do revise and get a poor grade, that's a terrible sort of situation.

Academic success, Craig maintained, was often an unknown quantity for white working-class males. If they did succeed academically, what then? He felt that there was often no one to explain to these young men that going on to further and higher education was an option for them:

> I see a fear of trying, the fear of doing something unknown ... I think it is a lack of aspiration for young working-class boys. I think ... there is no established tradition of going into academia for working-class boys because they always did what

their dad did ... in the mines or something like that. That has gone now ... And there is a great deal of disenchantment ... a resignation ... No one I know has been to university so I am not going to go to university ... it is not cool. There is not the money, there is not the support, and there is not the established tradition of it in the white working-class communities.

Frank echoed similar sentiments:

They feel that they are in a lower class so they are going to finish in the lower class ... you're always going to get the people that are just going to give up straight away, too scared to try anything.

Harvey recounts that for some of the white working-class young men he was at school with: 'There is just no motivation especially academically, English and maths and stuff, they just don't want to do it. They just don't find it interesting.'

Frank, too, felt that one of the issues for people coming from a similar background to himself was that: 'People aren't getting the motivation. They are just thinking I'll just get through school, I'm not going to do very well and will just fail, just drop out and get a job.' Adam informed me that in the area he was from:

It's just the norm [to under-achieve academically] and people don't aspire to do anything more than they are required to. People all want to leave school when they are 16, just get a job around and then their kids will do the same ... so my area isn't the best for employability or academically.

Nathan said that in his experience many white working-class boys did not enjoy school and they 'were dying to get out of school ... they couldn't wait to leave to have freedom'.

Could the behaviours exhibited by the young men who are not seen as academic be self-protective behaviours, as postulated by Covington (1992) and presented as a 'self-worth theory', which holds that some students are motivated to protect their sense of self-worth rather than make a risky attempt to succeed academically? Academically successful students value academic ability, whereas students who do not see themselves as academic may engage in failure-avoidance techniques, with education sidelined in favour of street culture, contemporary music, sports, and being with like-minded peers (Stahl, 2015). These behaviours protect the boys' self-worth.

John raises the issue of teachers' lack of aspirations and expectations for some white working-class boys:

> To be honest they could do a lot better than they were doing, I don't think the teachers helped a lot of the time because they just sort of ... once they had lowered their aspirations themselves of the pupils they just sort of matched that and thought 'right okay, we'll aim for the C grade if we can or lower', something like that a lot of the time.

Craig, who became a teacher, suggested that:

> Even these people who disrupt in lessons, even these people who resign themselves, they know somewhere back there, I am convinced they know that there has got to be something better than this. That is what I try to encourage. You know if you think that, if you think there is that one niggling bit of feeling in your head that you are not happy with the way you are, with what you are doing with your life, change it, because you can. Don't let anything hold you back.

What the young men iterated was that teachers play an important role in igniting the academic spark in students from a white working-class background when they first arrive at school. Teachers play an equally vital role in keeping that spark alive. It is the teacher's role to maintain their students' interest in a pro-school culture.

Leon raised the issue of funding and the wider material context of people's lives:

> I think saying to everyone you should be applying to a good university and you can all get in if you work hard by trying just ignores the realities of people's wider lives ... I think we can firstly make sure that education is funded correctly and that people are funded correctly.

For some white working-class young men, home life can be very complicated. Some of them may be caring for an ill member of the family, the economic situation may be difficult at home, and their living conditions may be a problem. Leon is suggesting these factors need to be considered before a child can be expected to achieve academic success.

Leon then went on to say that he thought schools should ensure:

That just ordinary people who want to come to school, do a decent amount and then just go away, aren't disrupted by others or [if they] aren't really talented, don't kind of get pushed into a filter. I think it is hard though, I think teaching is an impossible job and I don't envy them at all.

Leon believes that all children are entitled to a good basic education equitably delivered, but that it is not realistic to expect everyone in society to go on to higher education.

Football: A substitute for education?

Seven of the young men I interviewed chose to study sports science at university, not only because of their love of sport and particularly football (except in Frank's case – his chosen sport was rugby), but also because they had had an inspirational PE teacher at some stage in their school career. They all played football or rugby in some form throughout their university careers. While they had managed to combine their love of sport and academic study, they commented that football often took precedence over schoolwork (for many working-class boys). Craig explained that boys and under-achievement is very much looked upon a lot of the time as:

Oh, boys will be boys thing ... when boys didn't do well at my old school it was fine because they were really good at football ... Football mad, football, football, football ... Didn't get a very good maths grade? 'That's okay because I got an A in PE.' And there is very much a mentality of not addressing the real problem. It is a hope and people use it because they don't want to work hard ... Face the reality that you are going to have to work for your maths GCSE ... the ambition doesn't exist, the ambition is the dream ... Which isn't really an ambition. It is a fallacy, it is a fantasy ... So many people stumble through life ...

A great deal of research has highlighted the role of football in the lives of many young white working-class men. From the viewpoint of their peers, the boys who were good at football were seen as 'cool' (Power *et al.*, 1998). Football prowess proves that young men are 'hard' (Smith, 2007). In an earlier study, I was told by Chris, one of the academically successful white working-class participants, that he felt very strongly that the major reason why many white working-class boys did not succeed academically was because they held aspirations of being 'the next Beckham or Rooney'. Many were caught up with this popular notion of success and they would then spend their time focusing on football as opposed to academic study. Dreaming that they would indeed one day become a renowned footballer with all the trappings of success that came with it, study and academia were irrelevant to their ambitions (Travers, 2011).

Success in sport has often been regarded by some young white working-class men as a substitute for academic success. However, the versions of masculinity that are on offer as resources for identity construction in higher education institutions may be more complex and more emotionally versatile, and may offer a challenge to some of the more limited versions that exist. Indeed, Gee (2014) refers to 'flexible masculinities', role models such as David Beckham who 'bend the codes' of masculinity. The young men who attended modern universities and studied sports science have shown this flexibility, drawing on their earlier cultures of masculinity to perform their emergent identities as young graduates.

Discussion

All of the young men in this study highlighted the central role of the family and particularly the powerful influence of parents in encouraging educational success in their offspring. The participants recognized that habitus plays a central role in influencing, if not determining, educational outcomes. It was possible, from what they said, to trace Bourdieu's claims about the primary habitus of the home and its role in establishing sets of conscious and unconscious practices around the importance of education and its capacity for social mobility (Bourdieu and Wacquant, 1992).

Bourdieu argued that the primary habitus of the home could be transformed into a secondary habitus. Schools and teachers' roles are fundamental in this transformation process. The young men had benefited enormously from their education, they had all had teachers who had inspired them, and their experiences at university had imbued them with confidence. However, the participants all reported some negative accounts of white working-class boys' school-based experiences. One point that emerges from all of the accounts of teachers' stereotyping of, and low aspirations for, white working-class males is that schools and teachers have a powerful role in transforming the primary habitus of students. By exposing them to alternative experiences, by encouraging, mentoring, and supporting them, teachers can be instrumental in changing their students' educational experiences. However, while this approach has been embedded in the rhetoric of policy approaches towards the education of white working-class young people (Sergeant, 2009), from what the participants had to say, not much had changed in their view and in their experience.

In this chapter, I have concentrated on some of the reasons for the long-standing under-achievement of white working-class males as detailed by the participants. Now I want to return briefly to issues of masculinity.

The literature (from Willis's work in 1977 to Connell and Messerschmidt, 2005) suggests that some forms of cultures of masculinity have been identified as simultaneously compensating for, and contributing to, the educational failure of white working-class boys. From what participants said, if the primary habitus espouses 'doing what dad does' and this occupation does not require any form of post-compulsory education, then white working-class males are less likely to be pro-education. However, in many of the working-class localities, traditional male occupations have vanished (for example, coal mining or ship building); thus, young men are being exposed to dominant forms of masculinity that are counterproductive as the jobs they privilege are no longer available.

The young men in my research who studied sports science at university appeared to have a form of 'flexible masculinity' (Gee, 2014) that has allowed them to use their sporting capital and convert it into academic capital. These young men have a primary habitus that has enabled them to be academically successful while at the same time working positively with some versions of dominant masculinity. They have bent the codes of masculinity and diversified the available options of masculinity – they have produced a flexible masculinity.

All of the participants saw themselves as more independent, with a broader outlook on life, and they left university secure in the knowledge that they had successfully broken the mould. However, while they had all achieved against the odds, they identified the dual roles of family and of school aspirations and support as fundamental to their success. As they all pointed out, the school has the potential to interrupt and transform the primary habitus to influence the academic achievement of white working-class males; the tragedy is that, in their experience, this is still just not happening in enough schoolrooms.

Chapter 7

Conclusions: Drawing the study together

I think everyone changes at university. You become your own person, you become independent, you know what you enjoy doing, you learn how to do things your own way.

(Adam, study participant)

Research intentions

White working-class males' academic (under-) achievement is of great concern in England as their academic performance at age 16 is lower than any other ethnic group. This area of research is often considered from a negative perspective but this book set out to contribute to this contentious issue by exploring it from a positive position, working with a cohort of white working-class young men who had done well at school and had all gained entry to university. They were afforded the opportunity to tell their life stories, which included their home lives, trajectories from primary school through university, and their career aspirations. The subjective lived experiences of these high-achieving young men were central to uncovering the factors that enabled them to experience academic success while most of their peers failed to do so.

As well as highlighting the factors that enabled their success, it also explores the hurdles they had to overcome. All of the young men worked hard at achieving their aims and, for them, it was a day-to-day and year-to-year commitment; they experienced disappointments, but they did not let these get in the way of their aim of 'going to uni' (Frank). Personal attributes played a part: they showed qualities of perseverance and motivation, and were agentic in their educational progression; through sheer determination they succeeded academically, and as agents they moved fields (Bourdieu, 1998).

The participants did work hard to achieve their academic success, but they also understood that their academic success was attributable to more than a meritocratic educational system selecting them for academic advancement. They equally recognized that their attainments were due to a constellation of factors, not all of their own making, and that arguably they have slipped through the net, while society continues by and large to reproduce itself (House of Commons Education Committee, 2014).

Theoretical perspectives reconsidered

As previously detailed (see Chapter 1), in analysing factors relating to family circumstances, educational choice-making, and cultural patterns, the work of Bourdieu seems highly applicable. His work is best known for its focus on social class reproduction; his concepts of habitus, field, and capital helped me begin to tease out and explain the factors that enabled the young men to experience academic success.

However, while Bourdieu's work proved very useful in my mapping of the factors involved in the participants' experiences, such as shifts in primary habitus and the role of field, the account that I have presented in this book is not one of straightforward social reproduction. My findings suggest that there are a number of key factors that together contributed to the academic success of the young men and enabled them to experience social mobility. Thus, there is a need to question whether Bourdieu's work explains how social transformations occur.

My sample were all from working-class communities and had all done well in their educational trajectories, achieving educational success against the odds. In relation to my Bourdieusian approach, this transformation was effected because of shifts in field (sixth-form provision, significant teachers) as well as in the primary habitus. These findings led me to understand that habitus is not a deterministic concept and that there is a need for a more sophisticated and complex understanding of habitus and the habitus–field interplay.

Research questions

This book set out to determine the answers to three research questions that framed the study. The core findings provide the answers.

How do academically successful white working-class young men account for their achievements?

The young men in this study explained that their mothers were important in providing the security and support that enabled them to engage with confidence in education, and their habitus provided them with a positive attitude to schooling. However, most of their siblings chose not to engage with academic study, even though they had, arguably, been exposed to the same habitus as their brothers. These findings speak to a habitus that is complicated, time-specific, and situated because, while habitus generates within the individual certain sets of understandings and practices, *agency* as well as changes in the habitus (such as changes in family circumstances) permit the restructuring of the primary habitus, producing a habitus that is *uniquely* individual.

Experiencing academic success early on was important. Many participants referred to teachers in those early years who had offered encouragement, and exposure to the social and cultural capital of their teachers through positive interactions was crucial. This resulted in the participants developing positive learner identities early in their school careers and these positive identities stayed with them throughout their academic trajectories.

Bourdieu (1990b) maintains that cultural capital consists of familiarity with the dominant culture of society and its way of being, that academia at all levels is a middle-class construct, and therefore that it is difficult for working-class children to succeed within it. However, the participants appeared to have acquired the social and cultural capital necessary for them to experience academic success. They successfully navigated their way through the English education system.

Most of the young men reported mixed experiences at secondary school because the institutional habitus of some of their schools was not academic. However, most reported that they had at least one teacher who inspired them to succeed and all of them successfully completed their GCSEs. This was a critical accomplishment because without academic qualifications at this point of transition, academic success, as measured by access to higher education, is much more difficult to achieve.

Beyond compulsory schooling at age 16, nine young men chose the traditional academic route of A levels or the International Baccalaureate, and six chose to undertake a BTEC in sport. On entering the sixth form, the participants discovered themselves with like-minded pro-school students and found that discipline problems were no longer an issue. All of the young men believed that choosing to continue their schooling beyond GCSE level was a signal that they intended to go on to higher education. Many of them spent three years in the sixth form in their efforts to achieve entrance to university.

The young men who chose to study for a BTEC qualification instead of the traditional A level subjects were limiting the number of universities they could apply to, as it is generally only the modern universities that accept BTEC qualifications; but they chose to undertake a BTEC in sport because they enjoyed sport and wanted to make a career for themselves in the sporting arena. Some believed that they would not have achieved the necessary grades had they followed the traditional A level route. Thus, they made a rational choice to undertake a BTEC in their endeavours to attend university to study sports science. Those who gained entry to elite universities explained that without the guidance and encouragement of a teacher, they would never have considered the possibility of applying. This highlights the importance of providing information and guidance about higher education to students with working-class backgrounds where attending university is not the norm.

How and in what ways do academically successful white working-class young men interpret their university experiences?

Having successfully navigated their way through the school system, the young men entered university. They all initially reported experiencing apprehension and difficulties in negotiating the culture and unwritten rules within the university setting. They did not have the cultural capital necessary to make the change from school to university life seamlessly. This caused some initial dissonance for the young men – a clear case of habitus and social field not matching. However, they adapted to this new institutional habitus: changing, even transforming, their lives over time.

The participants reported some differences in their university experiences depending on which type of university they attended. The young men at the modern universities found that university life was not so all-encompassing. Contact hours were fewer than in the elite universities, written work was required only at the end of each semester, and their social and sporting activities mostly took place outside university. Some of the young men attending modern universities lived at home and all but one of the others lived in accommodation outside the university. It was not unusual for some of them suddenly to discover they had essays to complete within days or hours of the realization. Many of them did not organize their workload over the course of the semester and this resulted in some poor work being handed in and, at times, the need to resit units of study. They also believed that they had to sort out their own problems, and this resulted in many of them not doing as well academically as they might have done. These young men were not as immersed in university life as their counterparts at the elite universities and they therefore took longer to come to terms with the culture and mores of the university.

There were also differences in terms of my participants' orientation to the labour market. The men who had attended the modern universities seemed much less focused on their future careers than those attending the elite universities. Despite this, all of the participants who had planned to go into employment immediately on graduating found work.

The elite universities provided connections that the young men could tap into to find suitable work experience in organizations, such as law firms and the civil service, while they were at university. This often led to future professional employment opportunities. These participants had access to the wider social capital and networks of the university, which enabled them to access the experiences necessary to secure professional employment on graduation.

What reasons (if any) do academically successful white working-class males give for the under-achievement of many of their peers? What do they think could make an educational difference?

As previously stated, some children from working-class backgrounds can feel alienated in school as they do not come with the necessary social and cultural capital. They find the culture of school unfamiliar to them, they can be made to feel inferior, and they are less likely to succeed in the school environment. Bourdieu (1984) believes that schools teach and socialize children in *distinct* ways using a certain type of language and that these in-school practices may act as forms of symbolic violence, alienating those from working-class backgrounds by failing to acknowledge, understand, and accept the cultural differences they bring.

Certainly, from the perspectives of the young men in this study, the school experiences of many white working-class males are less than ideal. They identified the practice of setting in both primary and secondary schools as having a negative academic effect on those put into the lower sets. They believed that, once children were put into the lower sets, their aspirations as well as those of their parents and teachers were dampened, resulting in many of those students giving up on education very early in their academic careers. They suggested that teachers held preconceived notions about white working-class boys, seeing them as lacking aspirations, not interested in academic pursuit, and not capable of experiencing academic success. Low teacher expectations were seen by the young men as the norm. Many also reported that teachers did not fully explain the benefits and the opportunities that were available to those with a good education.

Some school practices, as reported by the participants, make for sobering reading and need to be addressed. These practices amount to symbolic violence, and the misrecognition of social privilege is why social inequality continues to be reproduced. The young men identified and *recognized* what went on in schools and how this appeared to cement white working-class boys into a subordinate position. There may have been misrecognition on the part of the teachers, but there was little misrecognition on the part of the participants; they were clear about what they had seen and in some cases experienced themselves.

Core findings
Mothers are fundamental in providing security, stability, and encouragement to their children

Mothers were instrumental in their sons' continued engagement with education, providing them with the emotional capital necessary to engage with, and remain in, education while many of their peers were distracted. This is not to say that in all families it was only the mothers who provided this emotional support; fathers and other members of the extended families also provided the support necessary for participants to continue in their endeavours to complete a university degree.

The young men are 'gritty'

The young men persisted with their studies while most of their peers gave up. They understood the value of education and were prepared to work when others were playing, doing their homework when their peers were engaging in other activities. University proved even more difficult – coming to terms with the institutional habitus of the university and all that that entailed, as well as living away from home and working hard to achieve the dream of a university undergraduate degree, did not come easily to the participants. Economic constraints had caused problems for most of them, even for those at the elite universities where bursaries are more freely available. Many of these young men's home friends did not understand why they continued with their education and apparently sometimes taunted them about it. They have had to re-form their identities and have done this well, moving seamlessly between home and university.

The role of the school

This book highlights the important role schools can play in ensuring that boys from a white working-class background experience academic success. It is understood that schools cannot be held responsible for what goes on beyond the school gates and that they have children for a limited time; but the effect schools have on children cannot, and should not, be underestimated. It needs to be acknowledged that when entering school for the first time, not all students will have the cultural and social capital the school requires and it is incumbent on the school to make the difference for these students.

Schools and teachers need to be aware of the consequences of labelling and grouping children, and they need to understand the possible effect this can have on the aspirations of the children themselves, their parents, and their teachers. Bad behaviour needs to be dealt with as soon as it happens, but the question that needs to be addressed is: why is the child misbehaving? Is the child struggling with the schoolwork or, conversely, is the work too easy for the child? Perhaps there are issues at home that the school cannot deal with – but knowing that these problems exist is useful information.

Many white working-class students and parents have limited knowledge about higher education opportunities and benefits. It is imperative that schools provide this information to students. The dissemination of this information should begin in primary school.

Teachers matter
The young men had caring teachers who encouraged them academically and their experiences at school left them with positive learner identities. But they were quick to point out that not all children develop positive learner identities and that some school practices act as dampeners on the academic aspirations of white working-class males. Teachers should never underestimate the influence they have on children; they need to remember that a positive comment from them stays with a child for a lifetime, as, conversely, does a negative one. The participants vividly recalled the teachers who instilled them with academic confidence as well as those whose contributions were less positive.

University did make a difference
All of the young men found themselves highly employable, whichever type of university they attended, and all reported that they had benefited enormously from the knowledge and confidence they gained from attending university. They confidently moved from student life into paid employment.

Policy implications
My study does not offer a policy panacea to raise the educational achievement of all white working-class boys. Some of the individual factors that contributed to the participants' academic success cannot be provided by the state or by schools. There are, however, factors that are susceptible to education policy actions. These have been explored in this book and include:

- raising awareness of the symbolic violence encountered in schools by white working-class boys, which often goes unnoticed
- the discontinuation of setting of children, as this is detrimental to the learning achievements of those who find themselves in the lower sets

- ensuring that all children develop positive learner identities early in their schooling careers
- raising teachers' educational aspirations for white working-class boys
- providing white working-class students with a fuller knowledge of the education system.

One factor that had made a difference in the past was the educational maintenance allowance (EMA). Moves to restore this funding to support poorer children could be a useful policy lever for reducing the social exclusion that many young white working-class people experience.

The wider relevance of this study

White working-class boys' achievement has become a key focus of the education debate in England in recent times, with an inquiry being conducted by the House of Commons Education Committee (2014) on academic under-achievement by white working-class children.

Most of the young men in my study came from economically deprived backgrounds, but their mothers were able to support their sons' academic endeavours. However, often parents from such backgrounds do not have the time, or the will, to provide academic support for a multitude of reasons associated with a lack of economic resources.

The government's role should be to ensure that in modern Britain no family finds itself in a situation where survival is a daily struggle; those in our society who find themselves facing such economic hardships are in no position to spend time promoting the educational endeavours of their children.

The school plays a vital role in ensuring that each child develops a positive learner identity and that positive academic expectations are maintained. The university has a role to play in ensuring that first-generation university students are armed with the necessary tools to make a successful transition from school and home to university, as well as equipping them for the workplace.

This book then is of relevance to schools, universities, and the government and I close with a quote from one of the quite remarkable young men I interviewed:

> I think more than anything, university is empowering for someone like me because it has confirmed and expanded what I always thought was maybe possible. Absolutely more than anything, [what] I have learned here is empowerment. Really, a real sense of empowerment. You can do anything, you can be

anyone. But it gives you a way like nothing else can, like I say, the contacts, the people, and the things you pick up here, here and everywhere, you pick up tiny little things when you mention something, someone will know someone and this, what you don't have, this is what is the biggest problem for me, is that you do not have the social capital if you don't come to somewhere like this.

(Craig)

The young men persisted in their quest to obtain a university education, they showed true grit, and they benefited enormously from their education. I hope this book does them justice and that it goes some way to helping parents, teachers, and those in higher education institutions and in government come to a better understanding of the factors that contribute to the academic success of white working-class young men.

Chapter 8

Epilogue: Where are they now?

I do think I am fortunate, how lucky I am not only to have a job and, you know, a supportive environment, just to be very, very happy.

(Craig, study participant)

This chapter provides an update on 13 of the young men who participated in my study nearly three years after they completed their undergraduate degrees. I have re-interviewed nine of them and have been in touch with another four electronically or by phone. Two young men did not complete their degrees and I have been unable to follow up with them. I also return to the vexed issue of class and explore what we can learn from the young men's narratives.

The nine re-interviewed
Adam (elite university, engineering)
Adam came from a former mining village in Wales with a population that is 99 per cent white British and where 23 per cent of the population still have no academic qualifications. In the fourth interview, Adam reiterated how uncomfortable he had been when he first arrived at university because of his local accent: 'I could not understand them and they could not understand me,' he said. However, he quickly adapted to university life and went on to successfully complete an MA in engineering.

When he was asked about the class of degree he achieved in his first degree, his response was:

> Somehow, I managed to graduate with a first! And was also awarded the college prize for academic advancement throughout my time at university. Bit of a shock to be honest as wasn't expecting to do that well.

I asked Adam whether he thought there had been any cost to him in going to university. He replied that, for a long time: 'I felt like a massive imposter and that I was going to be found out. I found it quite difficult at uni ... I am quite comfortable in my skin now.' He went on: 'I think only positive things about my university experience. My department was absolutely incredible. I worked at two international car manufacturers, a food-processing factory ... the links to industry were incredible.'

Adam added that while he had benefited enormously from his time at university, he also had an advantage that he had not anticipated because: 'My background gives me an insight that other people don't have ... I see things differently than others ... it has helped me.' He stays in close touch with his brothers and mother, as well as his home friends, most of whom are working in some capacity in the village. He continues to move successfully between his home and his new world.

At the time of the fourth interview, Adam was in the second year of a two-year graduate programme with an international firm of consultants in London. He pointed out that the transition to work had not been without its hiccups:

> I love coming to work, it can be stressful and I sometimes work till 3 a.m. but I love it. But I felt quite lost moving to London, I was used to living in small places. So, I share a flat with two others but we all work crazy hours so we were never in the house at the same time. I felt lonely. But now there are 14 people from my [university] college living near me. It's great.

Our interview took place on the ground floor of Adam's place of work in the City of London. He had successfully made the transition from university to work but not without some difficulties, while his habitus was re-moulded and shaped through new experiences. However, he had once again successfully adapted to an unfamiliar world. When the interview ended and he strode off purposefully, I recalled the young man I had first met five years earlier who was full of self-doubts. I considered the changes he had undergone, the adaptions and transformations he had successfully executed in those years, and his parting words rang in my ear: 'Five years ago I never knew these places existed.'

Karl (modern university, education)
Karl lives in London with his mother and two younger sisters. He has always lived at home. I arranged to interview him for the fourth time, two and half years after he had obtained a 2:1. We met in a coffee shop not far from where he lived. He was very talkative and happy. He was working as a store manager for a charity although his aim had been, and still was, to work in the education section of a museum. His interest lay in developing

and preparing audio-visual educational materials. Karl was still optimistic that he would obtain a job in that field: 'The last job I applied for I got an interview so I am getting closer.' Karl's tenacity was admirable and he was full of confidence that he would achieve his employment goal.

When I asked if he thought going to university had been worthwhile, he was adamant that it had been a valuable time. He did not think that there had been any cost in going to university other than the financial one, which had yet to have any impact on him as he had still not begun paying off his student loan. Karl had not yet reached the pay threshold (at which point the process of repaying the loan begins) and appeared to be bemused by the fact that the loan was increasing year on year. He enjoyed his work, which he saw as an interim measure until he eventually found work in a museum, and he did not appear at all disillusioned that he was not yet working in his chosen field.

Karl had spent five years after doing his GCSEs trying to get into university, which he eventually achieved via an access programme. This showed that he was both resilient and patient. He was keen to stay in touch with me and he had a powerful belief that his university education would stand him in good stead in achieving his goals and in accessing his desired career.

John (elite university, PPE)

John came from a predominantly white British (93 per cent) town in the Midlands. It was once a manufacturing hub, but current employment opportunities are based around light industry, distribution, and technology. Some 27 per cent of the population have no academic qualifications.

John has always been a high achiever and he had driven himself relentlessly while at university, hoping to achieve a first-class degree. He had achieved a 2:1 and, when asked how he felt about his final mark, he commented: 'I am not overly happy with my results.'

At the time of the fourth interview, John was living back at home after five years away, three of which he spent at university, followed by two years in a large northern city where he worked as an analyst for a credit bureau. He has continued to work for the same employer since returning home, commuting each week to work two or three days in the city, then working in his home town for the remainder of the week. John had some serious health issues while he was attending university and these have persisted. He had hoped that by returning home his health problems would resolve themselves, but this had not been the case. Nevertheless, he had no plans to move out of the familiar environment of his home town. When asked about his employment situation, he responded:

> I think it's pretty solid for a first job, it is nowhere near as difficult as university, pays quite reasonably, and we'll see where it goes, [but] I want to make sure my career stays upwardly mobile and I don't just stagnate in this job because it's comfortable – but I can't really find anything that I'm genuinely interested enough in.

Unlike the other young men I had re-interviewed, John was full of self-doubts and he was the only participant who had attended an elite university and never really adapted to life there. When I asked how he felt about his university experiences, he said: 'I didn't like being there but I am aware that it is going to hold me in good stead for the rest of my life. I can apply for better jobs.' Although he found university life very stressful, he saw it as a trade-off: 'I genuinely didn't like going but … it's good to have something concrete on my CV like I went to [names university] for ever. So, you know, it's three years versus the rest of my life.' John was planning to find other employment within commuting distance of his home town. He explained that the reason he planned to stay there was: 'I just feel I am struggling to fit in anywhere else.' Some of his school friends had gone to university and he told me: 'Most friends have come back to [names town] living with their parents.'

The interview lasted for more than an hour and a half and John was very open about sharing his experiences. He was confident about his own intellectual ability and he understood that he had had an excellent education, but he appeared to lack some direction, which was not the case with any of the other young men I interviewed. He said: 'I have no passion, no goal in life, never really invested in anything. I never did.'

John appeared 'to be in the midst of a habitus in tension' (Byrom and Lightfoot, 2013: 816). Through education he had transformed his habitus, but class transition is a complex process and he does not seem to have developed an 'inherent part of belonging' (Bourdieu, 1990a: 67) within the middle classes. He has returned to the family home after five years away but he has secured middle-class employment. He sees this as a good first job, but in his own words, he 'wants his career to stay upwardly mobile'. However, this is problematic for John because habitus is in conflict with itself (Bourdieu, 1998), resulting in him being in limbo with no clear directional focus. John's class transformation is clearly associated with his educational experiences and occupation rather than with acquiring increased levels of social and cultural capital (Byrom and Lightfoot, 2013).

John's story is indicative of how problematic social mobility can be for some white working-class young men for whom primary habitus transformation is not straightforward.

Frank (modern university, sports science)

Frank came from a town in the south-west of the country. The main employers there are the retail sector, government, and tourism. Employment in the informal or casual sector is high, partly due to the impact of seasonal tourism. The demographic is approximately 94 per cent white British and 24 per cent of the population currently have no academic qualifications.

Frank took four years to complete his degree, obtaining a 2:2, and, on graduating, he became the education and welfare officer at the university's student union. In the following academic year 2016/17, he became the president of the student union, another sabbatical position. Frank, unlike the other young men who had attended modern universities, had fully embraced university life. He had lived on campus for the four years and had participated fully in university life, enjoying many extracurricular activities. He, like those at the elite universities, found university life all-encompassing.

Going to university was, according to Frank: 'The best thing I have ever done ... friends at home are in jobs that they hate, waiting for the weekend ... it is so easy to get caught in a bubble ... friends are just going to stay here for the rest of their lives.' When I asked if he felt he had changed because of his time at university, he responded: 'Massively, massively. Friends just go out and get drunk. I am looking to the future, to buying a house ...'

Having been at his university for six years, Frank now thought it was time for him to move on. Once his term as president of the student union was over, he intended to work in a similar role, perhaps in a trade union. He, like the others I have followed up, apart from John, was very confident and optimistic about his future. For Frank, going to university had significantly changed his life for the better and it was a choice he would make again.

On completing his undergraduate degree, Frank had taken a job within the university and had remained in residence on campus. His attachment to the locality, in this case the university, brought with it a sense of belonging, a strong social network, and a sense of security (Ingram, 2009); he was not emotionally ready to move. However, after six years at the university, Frank was applying for jobs outside the familiar university environment.

Leon (elite university, English)

Leon came from a town in North Yorkshire where the service industry currently employs 89 per cent of the working population and where 95 per cent of the population are white British. We met on a Saturday morning in a trendy coffee shop (his suggestion) in the town in which he was now living and working. He was immediately recognizable and already in situ. He gave me a very firm handshake and said he was delighted to be seeing me again.

Leon had obtained a first-class degree and had then gone on to a Russell Group university to do an MA in American literature. When I asked how he had enjoyed that experience, he responded:

> I found a lot of positives ... [names postgraduate university] had a more mixed demographic than [names undergraduate university], so I found more in common with the other students, both personally and socio-politically. It's interesting also to be on a large campus university, having been at a collegiate university and before that at school. I also liked living in a student flat. Basically, it felt as if I was having the 'proper' experience this time around. My only issue was with funding. I had to self-fund and it's extremely difficult to be full time and fit in a job as well. I was really struggling for money. This was an advantage of [undergraduate university] – the uni was so rich that they could afford numerous hardship funds and bursaries, which I benefited from. These were available at [postgraduate university], but competition was tighter and the funds are smaller.

After completing his MA, Leon worked for a year as an assistant librarian at a state secondary school in the south-east of England. When I interviewed him for the fourth time, he had just begun work as a graduate library trainee at one of the colleges of an elite university. He was very much enjoying his work and he observed that, as opposed to where he worked in the previous year:

> Here is much more cosmopolitan in that people may not agree with my points of view but show more tolerance, there is more opportunity for self-expression ... at the school I worked at last year it was different, there was a polarization of society ... it was traditional working class ... they had views on things that I don't necessarily agree on. I was quiet, I kept my mouth shut.

He suggested that while he thoroughly enjoyed his current post, he did have some issues. He explained that his job entailed instructing the first-year undergraduates on using the college library facilities and: 'It shocked me how many students were from private school ... that does something to me ... that says something about my [working-class] background.' Here, Leon expressed his sense of injustice that so few non-traditional students can access elite universities. He has found that the transition from one social class to another can be painful because, in his case, it is underpinned by a social awareness of how difficult it is for those from a background like his own to attend elite universities (Reay, 2013).

Leon was intent on completing the studies necessary to become a fully qualified librarian, which would involve a further year of full-time study to complete an MA in Library and Information Studies. However, he would also have to self-fund this study:

> As usual, the main issue is financial. Library school is expensive, and as I already have an MA, I am ineligible for the new postgraduate loans the government have brought in.

He was considering doing the course part time so that he could continue working and he was also assessing the merits of a distance learning course as this was a lower-cost option. However, he had reservations about studying online. As he said: 'Lots to think about.'

When I asked if there were any longer-term costs associated with attending university, Leon responded that other than initially feeling that he did not fit in, he did not consider there had been any emotional or psychological costs. He said: 'There was never any suggestion that I wouldn't go to university.' The cost, as Leon saw it, was economic. He was concerned about the level of debt he had accumulated. He felt a sense of injustice at the restraints he now encounters because of the state of his finances and he said: 'It makes me resentful.' But he was not letting this stand in the way of him achieving his ambition of becoming a qualified graduate librarian. We parted with Leon smiling and suggesting that we stay in touch.

Craig (elite university, history)

On completing his undergraduate degree with a 2:1, Craig returned to live in his home town, a sea port on the south coast of England with a predominantly white British population (92 per cent). Employers currently include insurance companies, central government, and retail operations. The fourth interview took place on a Saturday morning in a busy little coffee house near to where Craig lived and worked.

Craig had originally planned to go into the Teach First programme (an elite postgraduate teacher education course), but he was approached to teach at the independent grammar school he had attended for sixth form and he chose to work there. He undertook a two-year programme to achieve Qualified Teacher Status (QTS) while teaching in this school. Initially, Craig lived at home with his mother and step-father, which, he said, had caused some ructions: 'I get on my parents' nerves and they get on my nerves.' He has since moved out to a flat where he lives on his own. When I asked about his teaching job, he replied:

> It's a very rewarding job … just like doing a hobby … the school is very keen to keep me … I'm enjoying getting under the skin of teaching … I prepare the Oxbridge students, teach history from Year 7 through to Year 12 and I'm in charge of the history curriculum for Years 7 to 9 … I take it as a vote of confidence. I do think I'm very fortunate, how lucky I am not only to have a job, but a job in a great school, and, you know, a supportive environment and, you know, just to be very, very happy … I am empowered, I do want to stay in teaching because I believe that teaching is valuable.

When I asked if there had been any costs associated with going to an elite university, Craig said that while he loved the experience, he had also been completely overawed:

> I look back now and I had no idea what I was doing and I had no control. It was a whirlwind and I hadn't started breathing again till six months ago. I just felt I was carried away by the momentum of the place, of the whole place, the work was relentless, by the fact I was learning so much, not just academically, but about finances, about life, about finding out what you want. Trying to navigate my parents, trying to keep my independence and them at arm's length, increasingly becoming estranged from them and not liking that much. I felt just completely swept away by the whole thing … suddenly thrown in the deep end with very little assistance … when I go back I don't know, I find it such a bubble, you know, the type of people there, the cultures, you know, its eccentricities, which make it both brilliant and wonderful but also at the same time daunting and scary … I loved my time there, of course it works, it takes you by the throat. I always recommend it.

In all four interviews, Craig has always been enthusiastic and offered me memorable insights into his life. He remarked that:

> I have come to realize my strength lies not in writing, I'm not a great writer, but in speech. Which is why I feel that teaching, I kind of feel, it is my own. My skills do lie in knowledge and

things like that but actually, I've come to realize that I am quite gifted at being there and through the power of speech, being enthusiastic. Actually, getting them [the students] on board and bringing them along and chivvying them along, you know. Mr Motivator they call me!

Craig suggested that his desire to be a teacher had been motivated by the good teachers he had had during his own schooling. He pointed out that teachers were fundamental to the academic success of young men from a similar background to himself. He added that his longer-term ambition was to teach in a secondary school in the area where he currently worked and lived. He was motivated to teach young people from a similar background to himself: 'I don't want to stay in the private sector.' Craig's enthusiasm for his chosen career was clear.

Ben (elite university, law)

Ben came from a port city in north-west England where the service sector employs 60 per cent of the population and 85 per cent of the population are white British. Ben had attended a selective state grammar school and, rather than do A levels, he chose the International Baccalaureate (IB). He had been head boy at his school. He left university with a first-class law degree and had then gone to law school. At the time of our fourth interview, he had been working for 18 months at a leading law firm in London. He was completely comfortable meeting me again and appeared to enjoy the 90 minutes we spent together. He found living in London exciting and had adapted quickly to his current work environment. He was excited about moving to northern Europe on a six-month secondment and envisaged remaining in the law long term.

When I asked Ben how he now felt about his time at an elite university, he was extremely positive, though he explained that he had experienced some self-doubts:

> It was a bit, kind of, daunting to start within ... everyone sitting there from London and private school ... more about coming from the north rather than the school I attended ... a little bit of apprehension but I did really enjoy my time there and I tell everyone to go and yes the nature of the system means there is a lot of pressures etc.

He did not believe that there had been any emotional costs for him in attending university.

Ben appeared to fit comfortably into the working environment in which he now found himself; he was relaxed and very happy to be pursuing his current career. On parting, he strode confidently back to 'the office'. He had described himself as 'privileged', experiencing what Reay (2013: 673) described as an 'immense relief and gratitude at my privilege', but at this stage of his life he did not appear to have the ambivalence about what he had, or who he had become, that characterizes many of the upwardly mobile that Reay refers to.

David (modern university, sports science)

I met David for the fourth time in his home town in eastern Surrey. The population is 85 per cent white British and the main employers are the retail and wholesale sectors. The town has among the highest number of NEETs (young people not in education, employment, or training) in the country, but, overall, unemployment is just below the national average.

Straight after leaving university, having obtained a 2:2, David took on a teaching job with a private primary school near his home town: 'They gave me like, my own class. Just the sport side of things … then I was also a teaching assistant doing maths and things … the best job I've ever had!' He was there for one academic year and he could have stayed on, but he chose to go to Australia for a year. On his return, David said the school asked him to come back to his post. As he planned to travel again and was staying in England for only six months, he did not want to take on a teaching obligation, so he worked as a bartender and as a gardener.

His short-term plans were loose: 'I will just go with the wind.' Longer term: 'I really want to go into business with my brother. I want to do my own thing. I loved my time teaching but I really want to do my own thing.'

David was the only participant who, in previous interviews, had expressed doubts about the benefits of going to university. When I asked him this time if he had benefited from going to university, he responded: 'I don't know … you grow up as a person wherever you are, I would have, kinda, grown up if I was at uni, I uhm, would have grown up if I was somewhere else.' David was still unsure of the benefits of going to university some two and a half years after leaving. He explained that his mother had been instrumental in him staying in education: 'My mum pushed the whole uni thing and the college thing.'

David did, however, suggest that he felt different from his friends from home:

> Yeah very different, bigger I think, maybe, I don't know. Scary
> thought if I hadn't gone to uni that, yeah, I would just be like a

plumber or a fourth-year sparky … I do feel different, I do feel quite different from everyone around here, I don't know if uni did it. I want to make the most out of things. In a weird way, a little bit, just a little bit unsettled. I want to make the most out of it [life] really. I understand I am 23 now so not so young like any more, so I won't get the opportunity again, no like, serious girlfriend, no like serious job, I wanna go like to other countries, learn about their cultures. No one I know has done it. I've tried to get them all [his friends] to come along but no one is interested. They have got like their lives here, like they've got their girlfriend, or their jobs. Whatever, no one does it. Yeah that's why I think I am going to be successful when I … when it comes to it, but travel now is my main focus. But when I do come to a career, I will be really focused, like I will just work, like tirelessly, till I become successful. I think I've said before the money side of things isn't everything, but I've changed a little bit in that way in that I wanna be financially … just because it's like a game and I wanna win the game.

When I thanked David for taking the time to see me and we parted, he said: 'That's fine … cheers … weird just like time capsules seeing where people are.' A month after the interview, he was travelling again.

Graham (elite, physics)

Graham is from a relatively prosperous city in the East Midlands that has low levels of unemployment and where 75 per cent of the population classify themselves as white British. Major employers are the NHS and engineering manufacturers. For the sixth form, Graham attended a college renowned for teaching the sciences that was located in a neighbouring town. At university, Graham obtained a first-class degree and he is now at an elite university doing a PhD in Astronomy.

We met in the town in which he now studies. He was slightly late for our interview because he had recently had his bicycle stolen and had borrowed one from a friend. The borrowed bike was not in good shape and Graham had fallen off on his way to our meeting. Nevertheless, he walked in smiling and confident and when I asked about how things were going for him, he proffered:

It's wonderful when you get on and you know about the same amount as everyone else … lots of things the professors don't know … it's invigorating when you discover something that no one has before … no one has ever known before.

He did not think there had been a cost for him in going to university as he was still close to his family. He had been encouraged by his mother to attend university, and the sixth-form college he attended had a reputation for sending students to elite universities. But he did say that: 'When I first started [university], I felt inadequate. But I just worked and worked. I went from near the bottom to the top. I developed intellectually exponentially.'

Graham spent much time explaining what his PhD research was about. He had one publication in a peer-reviewed journal and had just submitted another one. He was very excited about the latter and explained that it was:

A big deal thing, just the thing that will set up my career, get me a post-doc … it's a discovery of serendipity … so I'm really excited about that. I already have one publication … I'm making a claim about a discovery … some politics come into it. I am analysing an old data set that everyone else had already analysed, implying they did a bad job and some people take that badly … the only reason I looked for it [the discovery] is because I was the naive PhD without preconceptions, so I just looked for everything that I could look for. So, the fact is that I am seeing something that shouldn't be there. It's a double discovery, really, really exciting.

He added that the field he was in was so new that he was the first generation to specifically train for it. He was enthusiastic about his research and it was a delight to spend time with a young man who was so energetic and motivated.

After we parted, I recalled the first time I had met Graham at the end of his first year of university. He was very quietly spoken, giving very thoughtful, concise answers to the questions asked. He did not make much eye contact and he came across as being very unsure of himself. The young man I had just spent almost two hours with could not have been more different. He was a confident, enthusiastic young man who was excited about his discovery and the new knowledge this would contribute to the scientific community.

The other young men

Ian (elite university, maths and computer science)

Ian came from a former mining town in West Yorkshire. The main employers there now are the retail sector and distribution centres. The population is predominantly white British, at 87 per cent. On obtaining a 2:1, Ian went to work in San Francisco as a software engineer in a high-tech company. He is still with the same company, enjoying life in California.

Harvey (modern university, sports science)

Harvey still lives with his parents in a large new town in Hertfordshire. Industries associated with light and heavy engineering, IT, and telecommunications are the main employers and 80 per cent of the population are white British.

Harvey had originally worked part time as a football coach. He now works as a multi-sports coach for a sports company that delivers national curriculum physical education (PE) lessons to primary schools. It also runs after-school activities in a variety of sports. In the written communication I received from Harvey, he told me that he very much enjoyed his work and was committed to continuing to work for the company for the foreseeable future. He said that he had no long-term plans career-wise and when asked whether he thought going to university had been worthwhile, his response was:

> Well, it certainly helped me obtain this job but my colleagues haven't been to uni so I'm not sure, but it will probably help out in the end if I do decide to change my plans!

Mark (modern university, sports science)

On completing his undergraduate degree, Mark returned to live with his parents in a seaside town on the southern coast of England. The service sector employs 95 per cent of the local workforce in the town and 84 per cent of the population are white British.

Mark and I have communicated only by text since he left university in mid-July 2014. On achieving a 2:2, he went to work part time at his old school as a teaching assistant and, to supplement his income, he worked in a bar at a sports centre. The following year, he took on a full-time job as a bartender and then went travelling. On his return from his travels, he went back to full-time bar work and wrote that he had:

> Taken a few [football] coaching badges to help with my teaching for when I eventually do decide to go into the 'real world'. I'm yet

to decide if it would be this year or next as there's still a couple of destinations I would like to see but my mum and dad are trying to push me this year. But it's been an amazing year!

The last time I heard from Mark was two and a half years after he left university, when he wrote: 'A lot has changed in the last year or so! I took a bit of a U-turn on my teaching and now work for a large international financial institution, kind of just fell in place.'

Edward (modern university, sports science)

Edward contacted me by phone nearly three years after completing his first degree. He was living at home in a large suburban town in north-east London. The population is predominantly made up of ethnic-minority groups with white British totalling 31 per cent of the population. The borough has the highest rate of low-paid jobs of any London borough at 21 per cent of the workforce. It also has a high rate of academic under-achievement, with 60 per cent of students on free school meals not achieving five GCSEs at A*–C.

Edward was working as a sports leader at a local primary school and was in his third year in that role. He was delivering PE lessons across the school to children aged 5–11, as well as taking before- and after-school clubs. He was enjoying his work but was moving to another school in the following academic year to undertake a School Direct teaching qualification (a school-led teacher training programme).

At university, where he obtained a 2:1, Edward had been ambivalent about the experience, but almost three years on he was much more effusive:

> Yeah, for me it was good, it like helped me mature more, for the learning it helped me a lot, like helped build my confidence ... looking back it was so like, so stressful ... like I didn't manage my time, but there were lots of benefits ... you know I only wish I'd taken first year and even second year more seriously.

Edward said that the sole cost, as he saw it, of going to university was the financial one and he could see only benefits in having a degree:

> It's a weird one ... [for] my job I didn't need a degree, but there is no progression ... I'm where I am, like this is it, no progression. I need my degree for lots of other things I've looked at, it's been useful ... I need it for School Direct.

His future aspirations included travelling and teaching abroad. He suggested he would do this after completing his School Direct qualification. He had posted a YouTube video and set up a website about adventure sports. He said:

> Weird ... I'm trying to increase kids' awareness beyond the screen ... funny how you change ... I had a mindset of being lazy, now it's all about maximizing my time ... now people are telling me I'm always doing too much!

Meeting the young men five years after the initial interview was inspirational. Their successes continue – however, as successful as they are, they are the exception among their white working-class peers (Strand, 2014).

A return to class

The concept of class is pivotal to this book and, while my sample is small, the young men's latest narratives highlight a number of factors that are linked to social class and fractions of class.

The young men's academic and career trajectories show how success in post-compulsory and tertiary education has allowed several of them to access professional careers, and though this applies predominantly to the young men who attended elite universities (Sutton Trust, 2016), one young man (Mark) who attended a modern university has also accessed a professional career. Mark's career trajectory is unusual as, generally, degrees from post-1992 institutions carry less weight than those achieved in elite universities, with most professional careers being occupied by those who have attended Russell Group universities (DfES, 2003).

I have been able to contact Mark only via text, so I do not know the details of how he came to access his career with a large financial firm. I do know, however, from my earlier interviews with Mark that he is an only child and that his mother (see Chapter 3) was pivotal in encouraging him to pursue his education beyond GCSE level and move on to university. His parents live in an Acorn postcode category described as 'Comfortable Communities' (see Table 1.1) and they could be described as coming from a fraction of the working class who are more privileged in economic terms than many working-class families. Perhaps the social, cultural, and economic capital available to the family has been a significant factor in enabling Mark to access his career.

Craig's family became more privileged in terms of economic prosperity when his step-father became part of the family. Craig's step-father understood education to be a route to a secure future. He encouraged

Craig to apply to a selective fee-paying grammar school for the sixth form, providing social and cultural capital as well as the financial means to enable this to become a reality. The family circumstances changed while Craig was growing up, opening up educational possibilities for him that had not been available earlier in his life.

However, not all of the young men who went on to access professional careers came from the more economically privileged fraction of the working class; two young men came from the lowest Acorn postcode, category 5, described as 'Urban Adversity', while three came from category 4, described as 'Financially Stretched' (see Table 1.1).

All of the sample understood post-compulsory education to have been beneficial. Their university experiences resulted in a broadening of their horizons. For example, Adam did not know that consultancy companies like the one he now works for even existed before he went to university. Many of the young men had travelled, and continue to do so, extensively. When asked if they would ascribe this desire to see other parts of the world as due to their tertiary educational experiences, they were unanimous in their response that it was. Even David, who always appeared ambivalent about the benefits of going to university, said: 'At the end of uni I was more confident, it broadened my horizons.'

In an earlier quote, David displayed frustration that his friends were attached to their locality. Working-class attachment to locality is well documented (Archer *et al.*, 2010; Ingram, 2009). For many working-class people, this attachment brings with it a sense of belonging and security. David's habitus transformation had resulted in a disjuncture with neighbourhood friends, as attachment to the familiar was not a primary focus for him. However, the disjuncture caused was not enough to terminate the friendships.

Several of the young men had undertaken, or plan to undertake, postgraduate studies, understanding that further studies such as a teaching qualification or an MA enhance their employability status. However, the financial costs of doing so weighed heavily on some of them and, as stated earlier, Leon was resentful that it was so much more of an economic cost to him than for many of his peers: 'Most other trainees are more privileged than me, they do not have the same financial issues ... a bit of me automatically bristles when I think about it.' Leon is acutely aware of the disparity between himself and his colleagues who have access to economic capital that is not available to him and to others from a similar background to himself. Leon's working-class limitations are not cultural but they are economic (Allen *et al.*, 2014).

Only one young man, Graham, has followed an academic route, undertaking a PhD in Astronomy. The reasons why only one of the sample chose to remain in academia in the long term is not an area I pursued, but it could be an interesting subject for follow-up research.

The class rupture that has been reported by some researchers (Reay, 2013; Skeggs, 1997) has not occurred with my sample. They have not disassociated with family; all have maintained strong family contacts, with four living at home at the time of last contact. They have returned to the family home, academically successful, confident, and positive about the future. Most of the young men have experienced some social disjuncture, but only John reported that it had been a problem and, as stated earlier, after five years away, John returned to live with his parents. He explained: 'I just feel I am struggling to fit in anywhere else.' John is comfortable about his academic achievements, but socially he has struggled to position himself within a middle-class context (Byrom, 2009). The others who have returned home see it as an interim measure, whereas John seems determined to remain within a familiar environment that provides him with security and identity (Ingram, 2009).

In conclusion

Seeing the young men five years after the initial interview was inspirational. Each of them had achieved so much personally; they were confident young men who were positive about their lives, careers, and the future. They continue to negotiate their way successfully, and seemingly effortlessly, around their multi-dimensional lives.

However, one fact remains evident: too few young men from a white working-class background access tertiary education (Sutton Trust, 2016). Social mobility for this cohort in society is a reality only for the few. As I argue in this book, teachers are fundamental to the educational success of white working-class young men, but for society as a whole to become fairer it needs more than teachers. Reay (2013) reasons that what is needed is a focus away from social mobility for the few, and more focus on increasing equality for the many. She argues, like Tawney (1964) before her, that social mobility focuses on the individual whereas, for a strong version of social justice to exist, there needs to be a focus on collective advancement. Perhaps the answer is 'to ensure that the contemporary working classes internalize a positive sense of their working-classness, one secured through pride, dignity and a strong sense of personal worth' (Reay, 2013). The young men in my study did have a strong sense of personal worth because they had experienced educational success, but this success should be open to the many, not just the few. Social justice, rather than social mobility, needs to be the mantra of the government. As Reay argues, social transformation requires a revaluing for all of society, placing social responsibility at its heart.

Afterword

Dr Bryan Cunningham

Two roads diverged in a wood, and I—

I took the one less traveled by,

And that has made all the difference.

(Robert Frost, 'The Road Not Taken', 1916)

Of all the insightful points made by the young men in Mary-Claire Travers's important book, one of the most arresting comes from Graham. Talking of the value of 'external people' coming into schools to help enhance pupils' awareness of different careers, he observed a dearth of such initiatives:

> Yes, that is what is really missing; you are stuck in the school system and you don't really know where it ends. And what needs to happen, the reason you don't know how it ends, is because *you get to choose how it ends*, that isn't something that we [white working-class] boys understand. (my italics)

The notion of 'getting to choose how it ends' is one that resonated especially strongly with me. As a 16-year-old, white working-class – my father and his father before him were carpenters; my mother's many and varied jobs included school dinner lady and postwoman – school leaver, I had not a clue as to where 'it', or I, would end, nor knew anything regarding the nature of Frost's 'The Road Not Taken'.

Of course, not all of Graham's, or my own, situation can be entirely attributed to our lack of information relating to possible 'endings'; myths (as alluded to by Meg Maguire in her Foreword) played a part, as did 'the poverty of aspiration of the working class', as Ernest Bevin was said to have once described the syndrome. Peer pressure, and masculinities, had their own deleterious effects, fear of failure came into the equation – and certainly factors such as the expectations of schools and teachers were, and still are, never far from sight.

The several real achievements of Mary-Claire's book include the thoroughness with which she elucidates the significance of, and interplay between, all of these matters and others. She does so through her highly methodical, balanced examination of an impressive range of previous, related, studies and reports and – to strikingly successful effect – through the voices of the young men in her study. Crucially, rather than leaving things with the 'is', she then offers the reader a number of glimpses of the 'ought' (as Barnett has memorably expressed it, the 'is' residing in the horizon of the 'ought'). She persuasively steers us towards contemplation of the nature of certain practical strategies for further enhancing the likelihood of our welcoming many more white working-class young men into our universities.

Progress has undoubtedly already been made on this front – but it has been at a frustratingly slow pace. A number of 'compensatory' steps have been taken to remove some of the litter of obstacles on the path to entering institutions of higher learning. Universities such as the Russell Group one I attended do now organize visits by 'external people' to local schools, many of which are in electoral wards with high levels of socio-economic deprivation, and as an alumnus I regularly receive invitations to take on a mentoring role. We have managed the quite dramatic expansion of higher education – for example, moving during the 1990s from a participation rate of 14 per cent to around 30 per cent, and subsequently to meeting Tony Blair's 1999 target of around 50 per cent of any cohort now following university, or university-level, courses.

However, as a whole range of statistical measures such as those cited in this book reveal, there are still variations in access – especially to elite universities – that are extremely hard to justify. We can possibly attempt to explain away the fact that few working-class applicants (and not just white working-class school leavers) go to elite universities simply by pointing to such truths as the financial worries for individuals and families that have burgeoned in a climate of austerity. There is, as at least one of the young men in the study describes, sometimes the issue of wanting to feel comfortable – 'at home', not 'out of place'. John reflects on his struggle 'to fit in anywhere else'. Of course, Richard Hoggart's seminal work *The Uses of Literacy* long ago explored these sentiments, and in my view the passage of time has far from rendered his perspectives devoid of relevance. Hoggart's composite 'scholarship boy' was, typically, 'marked out early' by his family:

> ''E's got brains ... 'E's bright', he hears constantly ... ''E's got brains', yes, and he is expected to follow the trail that opens ...;
> he is heading for a different world, a different sort of job.

However, we must certainly hope that, perhaps above all other things, our modern boy, following his success in the school system, does not then go on to 'be nagged underneath by a sense of how far he has come, by the fear and shame of a possible falling back'.

So, what else ought we as a society to be focusing on now, to ensure more equitably distributed access to university, and to our more prestigious universities in particular, and to be able to be more confident that the 'pool of talent', as Robbins expressed it over 50 years ago now, is being efficiently drawn on? And, equally importantly, what should the priorities be for ensuring that the kinds of anxieties observed by Hoggart – which at one point in his book he vividly describes as a *'tendency to vertigo'* – do not come to afflict our white working-class boys? (To use a rather ugly word, when, and how, will their success be *normalized*?)

There are a number of possible perspectives on these questions – although, to use another probably overused piece of language, it is unlikely that any one of these, in isolation, can be the *magic bullet* so often wished for. Basil Bernstein's much argued-over 'Education cannot compensate for society' (1970) has, over the years, certainly proved to be a useful starting point for my own reflections on class and educational achievement, and I would also want to steer readers of Mary-Claire's book in the direction of papers such as Gorard's, titled as above but with these amendments: 'Education *can* compensate for society – a bit'. Moving from *'a bit'* to *'in truly significant ways'* is what will take the hard work. This work will need to be a collaborative effort on the part of policymakers, academic researchers, schools, universities, mentors, parents ('More engaged parents can transform a child's educational prospects,' as Wigmore recently put it, in describing how, for instance, at least one study has shown that schools sending text messages to parents notifying them that their child needed to attend school for a test demonstrably improved attendance and performance) – and teachers.

In concluding her book, Mary-Claire reminds us of the centrality of teachers to white working-class boys' success. While pointing out that to achieve the goal of seeing a more inclusive cohort entering university each year, society 'needs more than teachers', they are, she says, in fact 'fundamental'.

In 1993, I was privileged to be in the audience for what was to be one of the last major lectures given outside his native Brazil by Paulo Freire. In inspirational and beautifully accessible language, he spoke of the personal philosophy that had underpinned his lifelong work in empowering learners. Of the many powerful observations he made, one above all has always remained with me – it was this: if a teacher were ever once to somehow communicate to a pupil that they had asked a naive question, then that pupil would probably never again ask a question in class. As our white working-class boys continue their struggles to understand, and positively influence, '*where it ends*', this is perhaps the lesson that ought to be indelibly printed on all of the 'week-to-a-view' pages in our academic year diaries.

Bryan Cunningham
Senior Lecturer in Education/Academic Head of Learning and Teaching
Department of Education, Practice, and Society
UCL Institute of Education

References

Barnett, R. (2008) 'Critical professionalism in an age of supercomplexity'. In Cunningham, B. (ed.), *Exploring Professionalism*. London: Institute of Education Press, 190–207.

Bernstein, B. (1970) 'Education cannot compensate for society'. *New Society*, 15 (387), 344–7.

Gorard, S. (2010) 'Education *can* compensate for society – a bit'. *British Journal of Educational Studies*, 58 (1), 47–65.

Hoggart, R. (1957) *The Uses of Literacy: Aspects of working-class life*. London: Chatto and Windus.

Lord Robbins (1963) *Higher Education: Report of the Committee appointed by the Prime Minister under the chairmanship of Lord Robbins, 1961–63*. London: Her Majesty's Stationery Office.

Wigmore, T. (2016) 'The lost boys: How the white working class got left behind'. *New Statesman*, 20 September. Online. www.newstatesman.com/politics/education/2016/09/lost-boys-how-white-working-class-got-left-behind (accessed 15 June 2017).

Appendices

Appendix 1

The Sutton 30

In 2011, the Sutton Trust developed a list of the 30 most highly selective British universities. These are, in alphabetical order.

University of Bath
University of Birmingham
University of Bristol
University of Cambridge
Cardiff University
Durham University
University of Edinburgh
University of Exeter
University of Glasgow
Imperial College
King's College London
University of Lancaster
University of Leeds
University of Leicester
University of Liverpool

University College London
London School of Economics
University of Manchester
University of Newcastle
University of Nottingham
University of Oxford
University of Reading
Royal Holloway, University of London
University of Sheffield
University of Southampton
University of St Andrews
University of Strathclyde
University of Surrey
University of Warwick
University of York

Appendix 2

Brief biographical descriptions of participants

Adam	Parents separated. Mother is a teaching assistant and father is a caterer. Has two older brothers. Attended the local primary school and local comprehensive, where he was head boy. Studied at an elite university and read engineering.
Ben	Parents divorced when he was 3 years old. Father is a copy writer and mother is a secretary. He has one younger sister. Attended the local primary school and an all-boys state grammar school. Studied the International Baccalaureate and was head boy. Attended an elite university and read law.
Craig	Parents separated. Father is a plumber and mother is an office worker. Has one younger brother. Attended the local primary and local secondary school where he was head boy. Then went to an independent grammar school where he studied the International Baccalaureate and was head boy. Attended an elite university and read history.
David	Parents are separated. Mother is a nurse and father is a planning officer with the local council. Has one older brother. Attended three different primary schools. Attended the local comprehensive and then a sixth-form college. Studied sports science at a modern university.
Edward	Parents still together. Both parents are council housing officers. Has an older sister and a younger brother. Attended the local primary school. Attended a Roman Catholic comprehensive and a local sixth-form college. Attended a modern university and studied sports science.
Frank	Parents divorced when he was a baby. Father is a taxi driver and mother is a supermarket manager. Has an older sister and an older brother. Attended the local Church of England primary school followed by the local comprehensive. Studied sports science at a modern university.
Graham	Parents separated when he was 2 years old. His mother is a teaching assistant, father's occupation unknown. Has an older and a younger sister. Attended the local primary school and then attended a comprehensive school out of the catchment area. Moved to a sixth-form college renowned for its maths and science teaching. Studied at an elite university and read physics.

Harvey	Parents still together. Mother is a nurse and father is a builder. Has one older sister. Attended the local primary school and the local comprehensive. Attended further education (FE) college renowned for offering sport. Studied sports science at a modern university.
Ian	Parents still together. Father works in the hotel service industry and mother is a teaching assistant. Has an older brother and a younger sister. He attended the local primary school and the local comprehensive. Attended an elite university and read mathematics and computer science.
John	Parents still together. Father has worked in a bank since the age of 15, mother works in a radiography department. Has an older and a younger sister. Attended a Roman Catholic primary school and a Roman Catholic comprehensive. He then attended a local sixth-form college and studied at an elite university, where he read philosophy, politics, and economics.
Karl	Parents are separated. Mother is a childminder and father's occupation is unknown. Has two younger sisters. Attended the local primary school and chose the secondary school because he liked it. Attended a modern university and studied education.
Leon	An only child brought up by his mother, a teaching assistant. Has Asperger's syndrome. Attended the local primary school and the local comprehensive school then a sixth-form college chosen because it was considered academic. Attended an elite university and read English.
Mark	Parents still together. Mother is an advisor in a job centre and father is a plumber. Is an only child. Attended the 'better' of two local primary schools and the local secondary school. Studied sports science at a modern university.
Nathan	Parents still together. Mother is a secretary and father is a bricklayer. Has a younger brother. Attended Church of England primary and secondary schools some distance from home. Studied sports science at a modern university.
Oliver	Parents still together. Mother is a teaching assistant and father is a builder. Has one younger brother. Attended the local primary school and chose the comprehensive with a better reputation. Attended a modern university and studied sports science.

Appendix 3

Mother's level of education and current employment

Participant's name	Mother's level of education	Current employment
Adam	Art college	Teaching assistant
Ben	Left school at 15/16	Medical secretary
Craig	Left school at 15/16	Receptionist
David	Left school at 15/16. Recently completed a degree in nursing	Nurse
Edward	Left school at 15/16	Housing officer
Frank	Left school at 15/16	Works in the retail trade
Graham	Left school at 15/16	Teaching assistant
Harvey	Left school at 15/16	Nurse
Ian	Left school at 15/16	Teaching assistant
John	Further education	Works in a radiography department
Karl	Left school at 15/16	Childminder
Leon	Art college	Teaching assistant
Mark	Further education	Business advisor in a job centre, made redundant in 2013
Nathan	Left school at 15/16	Secretary/personal assistant
Oliver	Further education	Teaching assistant working with people with severe learning disabilities

Appendix 4

Primary schools attended by the study participants

Adam	Local primary school
Ben	Local primary school
Craig	Local primary school
David	Originally the local primary school, then two others
Edward	Parents applied for him to go to Roman Catholic primary school but it was oversubscribed so he went to the local primary school
Frank	Local Church of England primary school
Graham	Local primary school
Harvey	Local primary school
Ian	Local primary school
John	Roman Catholic primary school
Karl	Local primary school
Leon	Local primary school
Mark	'Better' of two local primary schools
Nathan	Church of England primary school
Oliver	Local primary school

References

Allen, R., Burgess, S., and McKenna, L. (2014) *School Performance and Parental Choice of School: Secondary data analysis* (Research Report RR310). London: Department for Education. Online. www.gov.uk/government/uploads/system/uploads/attachment_data/file/275938/RR310_-_School_performance_and_parental_choice_of_school.pdf (accessed 15 June 2017).

Appadurai, A. (2004) 'The capacity to aspire: Culture and terms of recognition'. In Rao, V. and Walton, M. (eds) *Culture and Public Action*. Stanford, CA: Stanford University Press, 59–84.

Archer, L., Hollingworth, S., and Mendick, H. (2010) *Urban Youth and Schooling: The experiences and identities of educationally 'at risk' young people.* Maidenhead: Open University Press.

Archer, L. and Hutchings, M. (2000) '"Bettering yourself"? Discourses of risk, cost and benefit in ethnically diverse, young working-class non-participants' constructions of higher education'. *British Journal of Sociology of Education*, 21 (4), 555–74.

Archer, L. and Yamashita, H. (2003) 'Theorising inner-city masculinities: "Race", class, gender and education'. *Gender and Education*, 15 (2), 115–32.

Aries, E. and Seider, M. (2005) 'The interactive relationship between class identity and the college experience: The case of lower income students'. *Qualitative Sociology*, 28 (4), 419–43.

Ball, S.J., Davies, J., David, M., and Reay, D. (2002) '"Classification" and "judgement": Social class and the "cognitive structures" of choice of higher education'. *British Journal of Sociology of Education*, 23 (1), 51–72.

Bathmaker, A.-M., Ingram, N., Abrahams, J., Hoare, A., Waller, R., and Bradley, H. (2016) *Higher Education, Social Class and Social Mobility: The degree generation.* London: Palgrave Macmillan.

Baxter, A. and Britton, C. (2001) 'Risk, identity and change: Becoming a mature student'. *International Studies in Sociology of Education*, 11 (1), 87–102.

BIS (Department for Business, Innovation and Skills) and Sutton Trust (2009) *Applications, Offers and Admissions to Research Led Universities* (Research Paper No. 5). Online. www.suttontrust.com/wp-content/uploads/2009/07/BIS_ST_report.pdf (accessed 15 June 2017).

Bourdieu, P. (1978) 'Sport and social class'. *Social Science Information*, 17 (6), 819–40.

— (1984) *Distinction: A social critique of the judgement of taste*. London: Routledge and Kegan Paul.

— (1990a) *In Other Words: Essays towards a reflexive sociology*. Trans. Adamson, M. Stanford, CA: Stanford University Press.

— (1990b) *The Logic of Practice*. Trans. Nice, R. Cambridge: Polity.

— (1997) 'The forms of capital'. In Halsey, A.H., Lauder, H., Brown, P., and Stuart Wells, A. (eds) *Education: Culture, economy and society*. Oxford: Oxford University Press, 46–58.

— (1998) *Practical Reason*. Stanford, CA: Stanford University Press.

References

Bourdieu, P. and Passeron, J.-C. (1977) *Reproduction in Education, Society and Culture*. Trans. Nice, R. London: SAGE Publications.

Bourdieu, P. and Wacquant, L.J.D. (1992) *An Invitation to Reflexive Sociology*. Chicago: University of Chicago Press.

Brennan, J. and Osborne, M. (2008) 'Higher education's many diversities: Of students, institutions and experiences; and outcomes?'. *Research Papers in Education*, 23 (2), 179–90.

Brown, P. (1995) 'Cultural capital and social exclusion: Some observations on recent trends in education, employment and the labour market'. *Work, Employment and Society*, 9 (1), 29–51.

— (2013) 'Education, opportunity and the prospects for social mobility'. *British Journal of Sociology of Education*, 34 (5–6), 678–700.

Brown, P. and Hesketh, A. (2004) *The Mismanagement of Talent: Employability and jobs in the knowledge economy*. Oxford: Oxford University Press.

Brown, P., Lauder, H., and Ashton, D. (2011) *The Global Auction: The broken promises of education, jobs, and incomes*. Oxford: Oxford University Press.

Bryman, A. (2012) *Social Research Methods*. 4th ed. Oxford: Oxford University Press.

Burke, G. (2016) *Data on Total Investment in VET: What should be collected* (NCVER Technical Paper). Adelaide: National Centre for Vocational Education Research.

Bynner, J., Ferri, E., and Shepherd, P. (eds) (1997) *Twenty-Something in the 1990s: Getting on, getting by, getting nowhere*. Aldershot: Ashgate Publishing.

Byrom, T. (2009) '"I don't want to go to a crummy little university": Social class, higher education choice and the paradox of widening participation'. *Improving Schools*, 12 (3), 209–24.

Byrom, T. and Lightfoot, N. (2013) 'Interrupted trajectories: The impact of academic failure on the social mobility of working-class students'. *British Journal of Sociology of Education*, 34 (5–6), 812–28.

CACI (2014) *The Acorn User Guide: The consumer classification*. Online. www.acorn.caci.co.uk/downloads/Acorn-User-guide.pdf (accessed 26 June 2017).

Callender, C. and Scott, P. (eds) (2013) *Browne and Beyond: Modernizing English higher education*. London: Institute of Education Press.

Centre for Social Justice (2013) *Requires Improvement: The causes of educational failure*. London: Centre for Social Justice. Online. www.centreforsocialjustice. org.uk/core/wp-content/uploads/2016/08/requires.pdf (accessed 15 June 2017).

Clayton, J., Crozier, G., and Reay, D. (2009) 'Home and away: Risk, familiarity and the multiple geographies of the higher education experience'. *International Studies in Sociology of Education*, 19 (3–4), 157–74.

Cleary, P. (2007) *Motivation and Attainment in the Learner Experience (MALE): Final report*. Glasgow: West of Scotland Wider Access Forum.

Clegg, S. (2011) 'Cultural capital and agency: Connecting critique and curriculum in higher education'. *British Journal of Sociology of Education*, 32 (1), 93–108.

Connell, R.W. (1989) 'Cool guys, swots and wimps: The interplay of masculinity and education'. *Oxford Review of Education*, 15 (3), 291–303.

Connell, R.W. and Messerschmidt, J.W. (2005) 'Hegemonic masculinity: Rethinking the concept'. *Gender and Society*, 19 (6), 829–59.

Covington, M.V. (1992) *Making the Grade: A self-worth perspective on motivation and school reform*. Cambridge: Cambridge University Press.

Crawford, C., Dearden, L., Micklewright, J., and Vignoles, A. (2017) *Family Background and University Success: Differences in higher education access and outcomes in England*. Oxford: Oxford University Press.

Crawford, C. and Greaves, E. (2015) *Socio-Economic, Ethnic and Gender Differences in HE Participation* (BIS Research Paper 186). London: Department for Business, Innovation and Skills.

Crozier, G. and Reay, D. (2011) 'Capital accumulation: Working-class students learning how to learn in HE'. *Teaching in Higher Education*, 16 (2), 145–55.

Crozier, G., Reay, D., Clayton, J., Colliander, L., and Grinstead, J. (2008) 'Different strokes for different folks: Diverse students in diverse institutions – experiences of higher education'. *Research Papers in Education*, 23 (2), 167–77.

David, M., Davies, J., Edwards, R., Reay, D., and Standing, K. (1996) 'Mothering and education: Reflexivity and feminist methodology'. In Morley, L. and Walsh, V. (eds) *Breaking Boundaries: Women in higher education*. London: Taylor and Francis, 208–23.

DCSF (Department for Children, Schools and Families) (2010) *Identifying Components of Attainment Gaps* (Research Report DCSF-RR217). London: Department for Children, Schools and Families.

DeBose, C.E. (1992) 'Codeswitching: Black English and Standard English in the African-American linguistic repertoire'. In Eastman, C.M. (ed.) *Codeswitching*. Clevedon: Multilingual Matters, 157–67.

Devine, F. (2004) *Class Practices: How parents help their children get good jobs*. Cambridge: Cambridge University Press.

DfE (Department for Education) (2015) *GCSE and Equivalent Attainment by Pupil Characteristics, 2013–14 (revised)*. Online. https://www.gov.uk/government/uploads/system/uploads/attachment_data/file/399005/SFR06_2015_Text.pdf (accessed 1 August 2017).

— (2016a) *Participation Rates in Higher Education: Academic Years 2006/2007 – 2014/2015 (Provisional)*. Norwich: HMSO. Online. https://www.gov.uk/government/uploads/system/uploads/attachment_data/file/552886/HEIPR_PUBLICATION_2014-15.pdf (accessed 26 June 2017).

— (2016b) *Widening Participation in Higher Education, England, 2013/14 Age Cohort*. Norwich: HMSO. Online. www.gov.uk/government/uploads/system/uploads/attachment_data/file/543126/SFR37-2016_-_WPHE2016_01.08.2016.pdf (accessed 26 June 2017).

DfES (Department for Education and Skills) (2003) *The Future of Higher Education*. Norwich: HMSO. Online. www.msmt.cz/uploads/bila_kniha/DfES_HigherEducation.pdf (accessed 15 June 2017).

Dilnot, C. (2016) 'How does the choice of A-level subjects vary with students' socio-economic status in English state schools?'. *British Educational Research Journal*, 42 (6), 1081–106.

Dorling, D. (2014) 'Thinking about class'. *Sociology*, 48 (3), 452–62.

Dunne, M. and Gazeley, L. (2008) 'Teachers, social class and underachievement'. *British Journal of Sociology of Education*, 29 (5), 451–63.

References

Equality Challenge Unit (2013) *Equality in Higher Education: Statistical report 2013: Part 2 – students*. London: Equality Challenge Unit. Online. www.ecu. ac.uk/wp-content/uploads/external/equality-in-he-statistical-report-2013-students.pdf (accessed 15 June 2017).

Evans, G. (2006) *Educational Failure and Working Class White Children in Britain*. Basingstoke: Palgrave Macmillan.

Flood, A. (2012) 'Patrick Ness wins Carnegie medal for second year running'. *The Guardian*, 14 June. Online. www.theguardian.com/books/2012/jun/14/carnegie-patrick-ness (accessed 10 July 2017).

Foskett, N., Dyke, M., and Maringe, F. (2008) 'The influence of the school in the decision to participate in learning post-16'. *British Educational Research Journal*, 34 (1), 37–61.

Francis, B. (1999) 'Lads, lasses and (New) Labour: 14–16-year-old students' responses to the "laddish behaviour and boys' underachievement" debate'. *British Journal of Sociology of Education*, 20 (3), 355–71.

Gee, S. (2014) 'Bending the codes of masculinity: David Beckham and flexible masculinity in the new millennium'. *Sport in Society*, 17 (7), 917–36.

Gewirtz, S., Ball, S.J., and Bowe, R. (1995) *Markets, Choice and Equity in Education*. Buckingham: Open University Press.

Granfield, R. (1991) 'Making it by faking it: Working-class students in an elite academic environment'. *Journal of Contemporary Ethnography*, 20 (3), 331–51.

Green, F. and Zhu, Y. (2010) 'Overqualification, job dissatisfaction, and increasing dispersion in the returns to graduate education'. *Oxford Economic Papers*, 62 (4), 740–63.

Grenfell, M. and James, D. (eds) (1998) *Bourdieu and Education: Acts of practical theory*. London: Falmer Press.

Griffiths, D.S., Winstanley, D., and Gabriel, Y. (2005) 'Learning shock: The trauma of return to formal learning'. *Management Learning*, 36 (3), 275–97.

Hallam, S. and Parsons, S. (2013) 'Prevalence of streaming in UK primary schools: Evidence from the Millennium Cohort Study'. *British Educational Research Journal*, 39 (3), 514–44.

Hayton, A. and Paczuska, A. (eds) (2002) *Access, Participation and Higher Education: Policy and practice*. London: Kogan Page.

HEFCE (Higher Education Funding Council for England) (2013) *Non-Continuation Rates at English HEIs: Trends for entrants 2005–06 to 2010–11* (Issues Paper 2013/07). London: HEFCE. Online. www.hefce.ac.uk/media/hefce/content/pubs/2013/201307/Non-continuation%20rates%20at%20English%20HEIs.pdf (accessed 15 June 2017).

HESA (Higher Education Statistics Agency) (2013) 'Table T3a – Non-continuation following year of entry: Full-time first degree entrants 2010/11'. Online. www. hesa.ac.uk/data-and-analysis/performance-indicators/releases/2011-12-non-continuation (accessed 15 June 2017).

Hills, J., Brewer, M., Jenkins, S., Lister, R., Lupton, R., Machin, S., Mills, C., Modood, T., Rees, T., and Riddell, S. (2010) *An Anatomy of Economic Inequality in the UK – Summary: Report of the National Equality Panel* (CASE Report 60). London: Government Equalities Office. Online. http://sticerd.lse. ac.uk/dps/case/cr/CASEreport60_summary.pdf (accessed 4 March 2011).

Hodgen, J. (2011) 'Setting, streaming and mixed ability teaching'. In Dillon, J. and Maguire, M. (eds) *Becoming a Teacher: Issues in secondary education*. 4th ed. Maidenhead: Open University Press, 210–21.

Holdsworth, C. (2006) '"Don't you think you're missing out, living at home?" Student experiences and residential transitions'. *Sociological Review*, 54 (3), 495–519.

House of Commons Education Committee (2014) *Underachievement in Education by White Working Class Children: First report of session 2014–15*. London: The Stationery Office. Online. www.publications.parliament.uk/pa/cm201415/cmselect/cmeduc/142/142.pdf (accessed 15 June 2017).

Hutchings, M. and Archer, L. (2001) '"Higher than Einstein": Constructions of going to university among working-class non-participants'. *Research Papers in Education*, 16 (1), 69–91.

Ingram, N. (2009) 'Working-class boys, educational success and the misrecognition of working-class culture'. *British Journal of Sociology of Education*, 30 (4), 421–34.

— (2011) 'Within school and beyond the gate: The complexities of being educationally successful and working class'. *Sociology*, 45 (2), 287–302.

Ireson, J. and Hallam, S. (2009) 'Academic self-concepts in adolescence: Relations with achievement and ability grouping in schools'. *Learning and Instruction*, 19 (3), 201–13.

Jackson, B. and Marsden, D. (1966) *Education and the Working Class*. Harmondsworth: Penguin Books.

Jacobi, M. (1991) 'Mentoring and undergraduate academic success: A literature review'. *Review of Educational Research*, 61 (4), 505–32.

Jones, O. (2012) *Chavs: The demonization of the working class*. London: Verso.

Kvale, S. (1996) *InterViews: An introduction to qualitative research interviewing*. Thousand Oaks, CA: SAGE Publications.

Lehmann, W. (2007) '"I just didn't feel like I fit in": The role of habitus in university dropout decisions'. *Canadian Journal of Higher Education*, 37 (2), 89–110.

— (2012) 'Extra-credential experiences and social closure: Working-class students at university'. *British Educational Research Journal*, 38 (2), 203–18.

Maguire, M. (1997) 'Missing links: Working-class women of Irish descent'. In Mahony, P. and Zmroczek, C. (eds) *Class Matters: 'Working-class' women's perspectives on social class*. London: Taylor and Francis, 87–100.

— (2005) 'Textures of class in the context of schooling: The perceptions of a "class-crossing" teacher'. *Sociology*, 39 (3), 427–43.

— (2009) 'New adulthood, youth and identity'. In te Riele, K. (ed.) *Making Schools Different: Alternative approaches to educating young people*. London: SAGE Publications, 31–9.

Maton, K. (2008) 'Habitus'. In Grenfell, M. (ed.) *Pierre Bourdieu: Key concepts*. Stocksfield: Acumen Publishing, 49–66.

NAO (National Audit Office) (2007) *Staying the Course: The retention of students in higher education* (NAO Report HC 616). London: The Stationery Office. Online. www.nao.org.uk/wp-content/uploads/2007/07/0607616.pdf (accessed 15 June 2017).

Office for National Statistics (2013) 'Graduates in the UK labour market: 2013'. Online. www.ons.gov.uk/employmentandlabourmarket/ peopleinwork/employmentandemployeetypes/articles/ graduatesintheuklabourmarket/2013-11-19 (accessed 15 April 2017).

Ofsted (2008) *Sustaining Improvement: The journey from special measures*. Online. http://webarchive.nationalarchives.gov.uk/20141124154759/http:/ www.ofsted.gov.uk/resources/sustaining-improvement-journey-special-measures (accessed 26 June 2017).

Power, S., Edwards, T., Whitty, G., and Wigfall, V. (2003) *Education and the Middle Class*. Buckingham: Open University Press.

Power, S., Whitty, G., Edwards, T., and Wigfall, V. (1998) 'Schoolboys and schoolwork: Gender identification and academic achievement'. *International Journal of Inclusive Education*, 2 (2), 135–53.

Quinn, J. (2013) *Drop-Out and Completion in Higher Education in Europe among Students from Under-Represented Groups*. Brussels: European Commission. Online. http://nesetweb.eu/wp-content/uploads/2015/09/2013-Drop-out-and-Completion-in-Higher-Education-in-Europe-among-students-from-under-represented-groups.pdf (accessed 15 June 2017).

Quinn, J., Thomas, L., Slack, K., Casey, L., Thexton, W., and Noble, J. (2006) 'Lifting the hood: Lifelong learning and young, white, provincial working-class masculinities'. *British Educational Research Journal*, 32 (5), 735–50.

Ramaswami, A. and Dreher, G.F. (2007) 'The benefits associated with workplace mentoring relationships'. In Allen, T.D. and Eby, L.T. (eds) *The Blackwell Handbook of Mentoring: A multiple perspectives approach*. Oxford: Blackwell, 211–31.

Reay, D. (1998a) *Class Work: Mothers' involvement in their children's primary schooling*. London: UCL Press.

— (1998b) 'Rethinking social class: Qualitative perspectives on class and gender'. *Sociology*, 32 (2), 259–75.

— (2005) 'Doing the dirty work of social class? Mothers' work in support of their children's schooling'. *Sociological Review*, 53 (Supplement s2), 104–15.

— (2013) 'Social mobility, a panacea for austere times: Tales of emperors, frogs, and tadpoles'. *British Journal of Sociology of Education*, 34 (5–6), 660–77.

Reay, D., Crozier, G., and Clayton, J. (2009) '"Strangers in paradise"? Working-class students in elite universities'. *Sociology*, 43 (6), 1103–21.

— (2010) '"Fitting in" or "standing out": Working-class students in UK higher education'. *British Educational Research Journal*, 36 (1), 107–24.

Reay, D., David, M.E., and Ball, S. (2005) *Degrees of Choice: Social class, race and gender in higher education*. Stoke-on-Trent: Trentham Books.

Rollock, N.A. (2006) *Legitimate Players? An ethnographic study of academically successful black pupils in a London secondary school*. PhD thesis, Institute of Education, University of London.

Ryan, J. and Sackrey, C. (1984) *Strangers in Paradise: Academics from the working class*. Boston: South End Press.

Savage, M. (2000) *Class Analysis and Social Transformation*. Buckingham: Open University Press.

Savage, M., Devine, F., Cunningham, N., Taylor, M., Li, Y., Hjellbrekke, J., Le Roux, B., Friedman, S., and Miles, A. (2013) 'A new model of social class? Findings from the BBC's Great British Class Survey experiment'. *Sociology*, 47 (2), 219–50.

Sayer, A. (2009) 'Who's afraid of critical social science?'. *Current Sociology*, 57 (6), 767–86.

Sergeant, H. (2009) *Wasted: The betrayal of white working class and black Caribbean boys*. London: Centre for Policy Studies.

Sherriff, N. (2007) 'Peer group cultures and social identity: An integrated approach to understanding masculinities'. *British Educational Research Journal*, 33 (3), 349–70.

Skeggs, B. (1997) *Formations of Class and Gender: Becoming respectable*. London: SAGE Publications.

Smith, J. (2007) '"Ye've got to 'ave balls to play this game sir!" Boys, peers and fears: The negative influence of school-based "cultural accomplices" in constructing hegemonic masculinities'. *Gender and Education*, 19 (2), 179–98.

Smyth, E. and Banks, J. (2012) '"There was never really any question of anything else": Young people's agency, institutional habitus and the transition to higher education'. *British Journal of Sociology of Education*, 33 (2), 263–81.

Social Market Foundation (2016) *Staying the Course*. London: Social Market Foundation.

Spencer, R. (2007) 'Naturally occurring mentoring relationships involving youth'. In Allen, T.D. and Eby, L.T. (eds) *The Blackwell Handbook of Mentoring: A multiple perspectives approach*. Oxford: Blackwell, 99–117.

Stahl, G. (2015) *Identity, Neoliberalism and Aspiration: Educating white working-class boys*. London: Routledge.

Strand, S. (2014) 'Ethnicity, gender, social class and achievement gaps at age 16: Intersectionality and "getting it" for the white working class'. *Research Papers in Education*, 29 (2), 131–71.

Sutton Trust (2000) *Entry to Leading Universities*. London: Sutton Trust. Online. www.suttontrust.com/wp-content/uploads/2014/08/entryToLeadingUnis.pdf (accessed 15 June 2017).

— (2010) *Responding to the New Landscape for University Access*. London: Sutton Trust. Online. www.suttontrust.com/wp-content/uploads/2010/12/access-proposals-report-final.pdf (accessed 15 June 2017).

— (2011) *Degrees of Success: University chances by individual school*. London: Sutton Trust. Online. www.suttontrust.com/wp-content/uploads/2011/07/sutton-trust-he-destination-report-final.pdf (accessed 15 June 2017).

— (2013) 'At least a quarter of access gap to top universities "not due to academic achievement"'. Press release, 13 November. Online. www.suttontrust.com/newsarchive/least-quarter-access-gap-top-universities-due-academic-achievement-sutton-trust-research/ (accessed 14 April 2017).

— (2014) 'Teacher Summer Schools'. Online. www.suttontrust.com/teachers/teacher-summer-schools/ (accessed 26 April 2014).

— (2016) 'White working class boys have lowest GCSE grades'. Online. www.suttontrust.com/newsarchive/white-working-class-boys-have-lowest-gcse-grades-as-disadvantaged-bangladeshi-african-and-chinese-pupils-show-dramatically-improved-results/ (accessed 26 June 2017).

References

Tawney, R.H. (1964) *Equality*. London: Unwin Books.

Travers, M.-C. (2011) *Against the Odds! A critical consideration of the factors that contribute towards the 'academic success' of white working class boys*. MA dissertation, King's College London.

UCAS (Universities and Colleges Admissions Service) (2016) 'UCAS undergraduate end of cycle data resources'. Online. www.ucas.com/corporate/data-and-analysis/ucas-undergraduate-releases/ucas-undergraduate-end-cycle-data-resources (accessed 14 April 2017).

Vincent, C. (2001) 'Social class and parental agency'. *Journal of Education Policy*, 16 (4), 347–64.

Wigdortz, B. (2012) 'Teach First founder says effective teachers can break down the barriers to achievement'. *The Guardian*, 10 December. Online. www.theguardian.com/education/2012/dec/10/teach-first-charity-innovative-teachers (accessed 15 June 2017).

Willis, P. (1977) *Learning to Labour: How working class kids get working class jobs*. Farnborough: Saxon House.

Wolf, A. (2002) *Does Education Matter? Myths about education and economic growth*. London: Penguin.

— (2011) *Review of Vocational Education: The Wolf Report*. London: Department for Education. Online. www.gov.uk/government/uploads/system/uploads/attachment_data/file/180504/DFE-00031-2011.pdf (accessed 15 June 2017).

Yorke, M. and Longden, B. (2004) *Retention and Student Success in Higher Education*. Maidenhead: Open University Press.

Index

Index

Foskett, N. 18, 87–8
free school meal (FSM) pupils 1–2, 4,
    9–10, 13–14, 23, 41
Freire, Paulo 128
friends at university and at home 47–8, 51
Frost, Robert 126
funding for education 95
further education (FE) 19, 35–6

Gazeley, L. 86
Gee, S. 62, 97
gender balance in higher education 22
'gifted and talented' programmes in
    school 28
Gorard, S. 128
government, role of 106
grammar schools 31–2, 40; private 32
Green, F. 80
Grenfell, M. 38

habitus 2, 6, 8–9, 11, 17, 22, 37, 40, 44,
    61; class-based 29, 48; at home
    19, 25, 27, 46–7, 61, 82–3, 87, 97;
    institutional 19–20, 35–6, 43–7, 49,
    61, 66, 87, 101–4; interplay with *field*
    44, 71, 100, 102; transformation
    of 81, 98, 100, 123; unique
    individuality of 101
Hallam, S. 89–90
higher education, expansion of 9,
    13, 16, 127
Hodgen, J. 90
Hoggart, Richard 127–8
homesickness 44
house buying linked to education 33
House of Commons Education
    Committee 106
Hutchings, M. 21

identity *working class* and *educated* 68,
    72; *see also* learner identities
immersion in university life 49–50, 102
independent schools 14, 16
International Baccalaureate (IB) 40
internships 52–3, 79
Ireson, J. 90

Jackson, B. 24
James, D. 38
job opportunities *see* employment
Jones, O. 85

Kvale, S. 8

'labelling' of children 12, 104
learner identities 11, 56, 60, 101, 105
lectures, number of 50
Lehmann, W. 77
'linguistic capital' and 'linguistic
    codes' 46, 61
living at home 20, 41, 44, 51, 67

locality, attachment to 51, 85–6, 123
Longden, B. 77

Maguire, Meg *author of Foreword* 126
maintenance grants at university 4, 10
Marsden, D. 24
masculinity, cultures of 22, 29, 34–6, 50–1,
    56, 61–2, 78–9, 83–4, 92, 97–8
massification of higher education 13–15
'meaningful others' 28–9
mentoring xiv, 28–9, 41, 92, 127
Messerschmidt, J.W. 98
middle-class *capital* (of various sorts)
    29–30, 33
middle-class connections and plans 4, 33–4
middle-class knowledge and beliefs 6,
    15–18, 26, 30, 34, 38
middle-class students, advantages of
    16–18, 20, 44, 46, 53, 66, 77
mobility, social xi, 13, 38, 87, 97, 100, 124
money problems 21
mothers, influence of 24–8, 31, 36–7,
    57–8, 83, 85, 100, 104, 106
motivation for carrying out the present
    study 8; educational 83; lack of
    94; of young people 22

National Statistics Socio-economic
    Classification (NS-SEC) 4
Ness, P. xiii

occupational expectations for children 17
occupationally based class schema 4
opportunity cost of higher education 17
'othering' 34–5, 78

parental choice 34
parental involvement in schooling 36–7
parents' education 27–8, 38
parents' influence 16, 25–7, 82–5, 97; *see
    also* mothers
Parsons, S. 89
participation in higher education, extent of
    13, 15, 17, 22–3, 127
Passeron, J.-C. 16, 46
peer groups 34–5
personal attributes of students 2
'physical capital' (Bourdieu) 75
placements 53, 79
policy implications of research findings
    11, 105–6
popular culture 92
postcode categories 4–5, 122–3
postgraduate studies 49, 123
poverty 21
primary schooling 24, 30–2
'problem children' at school 89
professional careers 79–80, 103, 122–3
public schools 46